Lectures on the Church of God

William Kelly

w. K.

Scripture Truth Publications

First published 1865 as "Six Lectures on Fundamental Truths connected with the Church of God" by W H Broom (& G Morrish & E Crocker), ix+257 pages

New revised (second) edition published 1869 as "Lectures on the Church of God" by W H Broom (& G Morrish), xi+259 pages

Third edition published 1873 by W H Broom

Fourth edition published 1876 by W H Broom

Fifth edition (no date) published by W H Broom

Sixth edition published 1890 by W H Broom (& A S Rouse)

Seventh edition published 1897 by W H Broom

Eighth edition published 1902 by T Weston

Ninth edition published 1904 by T Weston (& A S Rouse)

Tenth edition published 1906 by T Weston (& A S Rouse; & G Morrish)

New edition published 1912 by T Weston (& F E Race)

Eleventh edition published 1918 by F E Race

New edition published 1918 by G Morrish

All the above have the same number of pages, essentially reprinting the 1869 edition.

Reprints have been published in the USA by Believers Bookshelf, Berean Bookshelf, Bible Truth Publishers and the Wilson Foundation.

First paperback edition published 1949 by C A Hammond

Photographic reprint 1969 of 1869 edition by C E Hammond (*sic*)

Re-typeset and transferred to Digital Printing 2007

ISBN: 978-0-901860-50-7 (paperback)
ISBN: 978-0-901860-55-2 (hardback)
© Copyright 2007 Scripture Truth

Published by Scripture Truth Publications
Coopies Way, Coopies Lane,
Morpeth, Northumberland, NE61 6JN

Scripture Truth is an imprint of Central Bible Hammond Trust, a charitable trust

Typesetting by John Rice
Printed by Lightning Source

PREFACE TO 2007 EDITION

This edition contains the re-typeset text of the 1969 photographic reprint. The Synopsis provided in the 1869 edition has been restored and, to aid the location of page references to previous editions, the original page numbers are included in brackets.

To assist the twenty-first century reader, minor changes in presentation (but *not* content) have been made. The use of quotation (speech) marks has been updated. Scriptural references have been expanded to provide the full title of the book and Roman numerals have been replaced by Arabic, to facilitate ease of lookup. The footnotes, some of which are lengthy, have been moved to a separate section at the end of the book. References to people and publications have been expanded to assist in their identification.

In his own lifetime, this book was amongst the best known of William Kelly's prolific writings and was described as "a veritable textbook" on its subject. Over one hundred years later, it remains so.

The publishers commend this book to you. As you read, prepare to be challenged!

John Rice

LECTURES ON THE CHURCH OF GOD

Contents

LECTURES ON THE CHURCH OF GOD

Synopsis

(Page numbers in brackets refer to previous editions)

LECTURE 1: "ONE BODY"

Difference of God's dealings with His people in the past and present dispensations, 17 (1); Adam, 18 (2); Abraham, 19 (3); Israel as a nation, 20 (5); death and resurrection of Christ introduce a new thing, 21 (6); the body composed of Jew and Gentile, 22 (7); the cross, showing the complete ruin of man removes the barrier to God's free action, 23 (8); God's thoughts set upon the glory of His Son, 23 (9); first shadow of the Church's union with Christ precedes the entrance of sin, 24 (10); Ephesians 1 is then adduced to show that God develops His counsels of grace before mentioning man's sin, 25 (11); the cross not merely meets the desperate need of man, but unites in one body Jew and Gentile, 26 (12); a new man thus created, 27 (13); a habitation in which God could dwell, 28 (14); Christ, God's true temple while on earth, 29 (15); the truth of the one body claims the attention of all Christians, 30 (17); human and divine relationships, 31 (18); Satan's grand object to hinder the present operation of God in the saints, 32 (19); and succeeds at man's weak point in that man likes to be

LECTURE 2: "ONE SPIRIT"

LECTURE 3: THE ASSEMBLY AND MINISTRY

LECTURE 4: WORSHIP, THE BREAKING OF BREAD, AND PRAYER

LECTURE 5: GIFTS AND LOCAL CHARGES

LECTURE 6: THE RESOURCE OF THE FAITHFUL IN THE RUINS OF CHRISTENDOM

types of the day when the Son of Man shall be revealed, 207 (230); Christendom's danger seen in Romans 11, 208 (231); its non-continuance in God's goodness, 209 (232); its excision, 209 (233); its apostasy apparent from the first, 210 (234); the man of sin, and the Man of righteousness, 211 (235); Antichrist, 211 (236); Cain, Balaam, Core, 212 (237); he who defends Christendom, gives the Lord the lie, 214 (238); deprecation of the apology, that the Lord will set all right, 215 (239); unsparing judgment His action when He comes, 215 (239); the Lord's provision for the faithful in the dark day, 216 (240); the Lord's own weight of authority attached to "two or three" gathered to His name, 217 (242); no wonder men shrink from Church discipline, seeing how it has been abused, 218 (243); the duty of a believer, to renounce every tie not connected with Christ, 219 (244); which is best, your rules or God's word?, 220 (245); how is it that the doctrines of men have taken the place of the word of God?, 220 (246); electing a minister, wholly at variance with Scripture, 221 (247); evils resulting from the dissenting and parochial systems, 222 (247); advice to saints taking their place with the "two or three", 223 (249); how to detect and exclude what is not of God, 224 (250); the great house, and who to separate from, 224 (251); "He that departeth from evil maketh himself a prey", 225 (251); "The Christian world", or evil with the name of Christ attached to it, 226 (252); trusting the Lord for eternal life, and denying Him for a bit of bread, 227 (254); what to flee and what to follow (2 Timothy 2), 228 (255); Christ addresses Himself to hearts, grieved at the dishonour done to His grace and truth, 229 (256); illustration of a rightly and wrongly constituted assembly, 230 (257); Christ the centre and rallying point, 230 (258); no ground for fear, if the Lord be the helper, 231 (258); conclusion.

LECTURES ON THE CHURCH OF GOD

Lecture 1:
"One Body"

EPHESIANS 4

The subject on which, with the Lord's help, I propose to enter to-night is the one body, the body of Christ; and this too not only as a great doctrine which the Holy Ghost has laid down with the utmost clearness, and throughout a considerable part of the New Testament, but also, as far as I am able in a short space, deducing some of its practical consequences, and showing its bearing upon the communion and the conduct of every member of it, that is, of every Christian.

But in order to develop the special characteristics of Christ's body, it will be necessary to explain how it differed from that which God revealed or set up in past dispensations; for there are distinctions, and even contrasts, between the past dealings of God and that which He is now accomplishing to the honour of His beloved Son. While there was of course always the only true God: while He had in times past those He loved upon earth; while He ever wrought by His Spirit; while there was necessarily faith at work in order to the blessing of souls; yet for all that there are essential and deeply

17

important differences, which none can overlook without loss to himself, without sure weakening of his testimony to others, and, above all, without coming short of the just perception of what God Himself has nearest to His own heart—His own glory in Christ.

Now it is perfectly plain, if we take up the Old Testament, that when man fell into sin God gave certain revelations of blessing, all of which find their centre in the Lord Jesus. We see this from the very beginning of Genesis. When sin entered, not only righteous government but grace instantly followed. God was there; and in the presence of the guilty pair, and in defiance of the serpent, the mercy of God spoke of that same blessed One of whom we are about to hear further and deeper glories. In due time God brought out, in a distinct and personal manner, blessings in connexion with Abraham and his seed. There we have the domain of promise— not only revelation of mercy, but distinct promise—to a given person and to his seed. This had not been the case in the garden of Eden. Man fell there; and it is evident that fallen man could not possibly be the object of the promise of God. There are promises *for* such: there could not be a promise *to* such. When Abraham received the promise, he was not a fallen man merely but a believing man. It was as one elect, called, and faithful, that God made him the depositary of promise. But it was when Adam fell, before there was anything of the operation of divine grace in him; it was when he and Eve had completely separated themselves from God, that mercy, entirely irrespective of their condition or desert, held out a revelation of grace in the person of Christ. The woman's Seed was presented more particularly as the destroyer of him that had wrought this deep and, as far as it went, irreparable mischief—irreparable to the creature, but only furnishing the opportunity for God to bring out His own grace to the glory of Him who, bruised Himself, was to bruise the serpent's head.

The effect of the promise to Abraham was that a family was set apart unto God, and, in due time, a nation. Next, we find that, as this nation was full of confidence in its own powers, God was pleased, in the wisdom of His ways, to try them by the law, as we all know, given at Sinai. I need not enter into the details, but just state the general outline of the divine dealings for the purpose of clearing my subject. But the issue of that trial, however long God might delay, was not doubtful for a moment; for at the very mountain where God spoke, the children of Israel set at nought the authority and the glory of God, and bowed down to the work of their own hands: that is, the law, as a moral question between God and man, was overthrown from its very foundations at the outset. God lingered—long lingered—in patience, and meanwhile brought out His ways in every possible variety. The crowning experiment of all was the presence of Christ, the Seed of the woman, and the Seed of promise, too; for now came the person who answered to all the revelations and promises, the ways and types and prophecies of God. He came, in whose person was found all that was worthy of God, and that was suited to man. But the coming of Christ brought out the awful truth, not only that man is himself corrupt, depraved, and loves his own will, but that he hates goodness—yea, divine goodness—in a man. He is the enemy of God when manifesting Himself in the most blessed manner—in His own Son; when manifesting Himself, not only in power—for we can understand a guilty creature alarmed at holy power—but in perfect love, coming down in humiliation, putting Himself at the foot of man, beseeching man; for this is in truth not a figure or exaggeration of man's mind, but God's own word. Hear His description of it: "God was in Christ reconciling the world unto himself, not imputing their trespasses unto them, and hath committed unto us the word of reconciliation. Now, then, we are ambassadors for Christ, as though *God did beseech by us*", &c. His love beseeching sinners was the attitude of divine grace in the person of Christ. What was the result? That man proved there was no possibility of extricating himself by any means that God put at his disposal: that if it were a question of man's delivering himself, no matter what might be the mercy or the blessing, no matter how deep and full the grace displayed in a living person, man was too far gone—nay, so truly dead in sin, that, far from being won by God's love, he only took advantage of it, and when Jesus put Himself at the foot of man, he lifted up his heel and trod on Him, the Son of God. But if man thus, under Satan's malicious guidance, cast out and crucified Christ, God in the cross not only demonstrated His love (herein is love, indeed!) but wrought out redemption, a work suited even for those that crucified Jesus, capable of blotting out the foulest sin man was ever guilty of. God has triumphed where man did his worst against Him.

But this is not all. In the previous dealings of God, when He had given His law, God had separated the nation that was called out of Egypt—had marked them off in the most distinct and positive manner from all others. It was needful. Men might have complained that there had been no fair trial; the corrupt examples of others would naturally lead astray. God set Israel apart by their institutions, rites, ordinances, services, and His law; and by that law, and by those rites, He severed them from all others; so that it would have been sin against God for a Jew to have communion with a Gentile, no matter how godly and disposed to respect the law of God. No doubt there might be such a thing as being brought out of Gentilism, at any rate to a certain extent; but still, all through the system of God's dealings by His law with the Jewish people, there was the express and total severance of His people from all the nations. I do not speak of the abuse of it, working upon the corrupt heart of man against others—the pride of men's heart, who despised others because of their own divinely isolated position; but apart from the evil use that Israel made of their separation, faithfulness to God then required it, and His will was in the thing itself. God was proving before the whole world the painful and humbling truth, that let a nation have ever such mercies, ever such privileges, ever such wisdom directing their movements, outward and inward—nay, everything pertaining to them, the issue of all is increasing enmity against God Himself.

The death and resurrection of Christ introduced a new thing in every sense. Now, Christians admit this in general as to the work of Christ in its application to the need of the soul. There is no person of ever so little spiritual intelligence, who does not confess, with more or less clearness and thankfulness of heart, the all-importance of the cross of Christ for his need before God. There may be a scanty perception of the extent of the deliverance, an interrupted and feeble enjoyment of the perfect peace that has been made by the blood of Christ's cross; but there is no believer who does not in some measure hold it and enjoy it, and thank God for it.

But there is more than the sinner's need met in the cross; and I direct your attention to what the Holy Ghost gives us in Ephesians 2, as showing the place of the cross in the ways of God—not merely in the salvation of the soul. At the 13th verse it is written, "Ye who sometimes were far off are made nigh by the blood of Christ. For he is our peace, who hath made both one, and hath broken down the middle wall of partition between us; having abolished in his flesh the enmity, even the law of commandments contained in ordinances; for to make in himself of twain one new man, so making peace; and that he might reconcile both unto God in one body by the cross, having slain the enmity thereby." Now, it is evident from this scripture, that the cross is not only the basis of peace for the soul, but the foundation also on which rests the "one body" that God is now making of Jew and Gentile before Himself. And we see this most plainly if we only look back to our Lord's own presence on earth. He forbids His disciples going into the way of the Gentiles—forbids their entering any city of the Samaritans. Need it be said that it was from no lack of love? It was not that His heart did not yearn over the most reprobate of Samaritans; it was not that He did not appreciate the faith of a Gentile—He had not seen "such faith, no, not in Israel". Notwithstanding, they were to go only to the lost sheep of Israel, because to such only He was sent, and so were they too. Now, here we find at once that, while there was this perfectness of grace in Christ, the holy order of God was none the less fully maintained. Law claimed a state of things essentially different from what we have described in Ephesians 2. There was a positive barrier even during His lifetime, the very thing being formally prohibited, which, after He died and rose, was not merely a duty, but the delight of love, the only adequate answer in the saints to that death and resurrection. (See Matthew 28:19.)

How comes this to pass? On what is so mighty a change founded? On the cross. It brings out the worthlessness of man, and most of all, the worthlessness of favoured, privileged, religious man—of man under God's law. For if man under that law failed, what other law could avail? The law of God was the wisest, the best, the most holy and just dealing that it was possible to bring to bear upon man's natural state. And here was the total failure of man; and God well knew it all from the first, for He took care that in the earliest book of Scripture, and all through, embedded in the very law itself, there should be plain words as well as shadows, showing that man would sin, and that only Christ, by His blood-shedding and His death, could avail. The very first revelation of the garden of Eden is a witness of both. Faith had no other expectation. But nevertheless there was a full, patient, long-suffering trial whether it was possible to get any good out of man, in the dealings of the only wise God with man. And now it was demonstrated in the cross that all was ruined in man, and that the highest advantages, short of God's saving grace, brought out the ruin most distinctly. Now there is room for grace to work; and, beloved friends, it is upon this that it is my joy to speak a little to-night.

We have come down the stream; we have seen what man was when it was a question of his working for God: we shall now look briefly at God when He puts forth His glorious power to work, not merely for man, but for His Son; for oh! we never get the full blessing until we see this great and glorious truth, that God has at heart His Son—that God is thinking, not merely of a blessing for you, for me, for any of those that love Him—yea, and in sovereign grace, for those who love Him not, if they repent and believe the gospel—but that He has His eye upon Him who did all and suffered all for His glory, and has bound up that glory of God with the fullest, richest, everlasting blessing of all who believe in His name. And now, then, as the fruit of the cross of Christ (where we have the weakness of God, where nevertheless we have the triumph of God—God Himself coming down lower and lower still in love, not merely, so to speak, beseeching man, but laying all the weight and burden of sin upon the Lord Jesus, thereby meeting the desperate need of sinners by His Son suffering for them,) what do we find? That in the cross He has given the death-blow to sin; He has "put away sin by the sacrifice of himself", as we are told. But besides, by it all the distinctions of Jew and Gentile pass away, and God brings out that to which He had always looked onward—that which was in His counsels not only *from* the foundation of the world, but *before* it, and which consequently He had shown before there was a question of law, and before there was a question of sin. For it is remarkable that the magnificent type, which the apostle applies in Ephesians 5 to the mystery of Christ and the church, was brought in before sin entered (Genesis 2). In truth, it was a counsel that flowed out of what God was and is. It was God in His own love, even God working from what was in Himself. No doubt, the entrance of sin has given occasion for God to bring out His grace in blessed ways; but, for all that, we must ever remember that there were thoughts and counsels of grace in God Himself. There was that which He ever had in His own mind, for the revelation of which, no doubt, sin might furnish the fit occasion. But sin was in no wise the suggestive spring any more than the measure. On the contrary, we see God indulging, so to speak, in the activity of His own perfect love; at any rate, we see Him thinking of, filled with, working for, His own Son. And I think it is of deep interest to observe the fact just referred to—the shadow of the church's union with Christ preceding the entrance of sin and the provisions of grace in view of sin.

And observe further, that as just seen in the type of Genesis, so it is in the epistle to the Ephesians. Where is it that you have the counsels of God traced out? Is it after man's sin has been portrayed in chapter 2? No; but in the earliest verses of chapter 1, where God gives the richest development of the counsels of His grace, entirely passing over and ignoring in the first instance all question of man's sin, shame, and need. This we have afterwards and in the profoundest way. There is perhaps no part of the word of God which shows us the depth of human evil more than Ephesians 2; but this is not at all the first thought. Hence we find in the first chapter, "Blessed be the God and Father of our Lord Jesus Christ, who hath blessed us with all spiritual blessings in heavenly places in Christ, according as he hath chosen us in him before the foundation of the world, that we should be holy and without blame before him in love." And then it is only just by the way that the apostle alludes to the fact of their sins, and in a single verse (the 7th), where we read, "In whom we have redemption through his blood, the forgiveness of sins, according to the riches of his grace." With the exception of that incidental notice of the fact of our needing redemption, the remission of sins, you would not know from the first chapter of the epistle that the saints of God, these blest ones, had a single evil, or a particle of sin connected with them. That is, it is God perfectly acting from Himself, in and for His own Son; delighting in Him, putting honour upon Him, giving Him what was suited to Him out of His own resources of love, and hence boundlessly to the saints, the body of Christ, as the end of chapter 1 describes them. It is thus that the Holy Ghost is pleased to introduce these astonishing counsels of grace.

Then, in the second chapter, we have man's state looked at most thoroughly. We see him weighed and found wanting as in no other part of Scripture. We have him here, not as an active being, alive in sin, but as all over with him, *dead* in sin—"dead in trespasses and sins". He is, therefore, hopelessly lost and utterly powerless in sins. The whole case is closed against him; and it is to this condition of manifest moral death and subjection to Satan, that the grace of God applies itself, in His quickening, raising, heavenly power in Christ Jesus.

But, again, we find that in the latter part of Ephesians 2 the cross of Christ is taken up, not merely in connexion with God's counsels, as in chapter 1, nor even in view of their desperate need who are the objects of His counsels, as in the beginning of chapter 2, but in contrast to the previous ways of God upon the earth. He is addressing Gentiles. Was it not a suitable occasion for God to unfold to them the one new man, the mystery of Christ and the church, the body of Christ? They were hitherto ignored, evidently outside all that God had been doing of old. God had taken up a separated people and had tried them. The Gentiles were as non-existent, so to speak, before God. Not, of course, that the secret providence of God did not watch and work—not that the grace of God did not act as to individuals; but, regarded as Gentiles, they were outside. But now these are the very objects of heavenly grace; toward Gentiles the call goes out loud and large. Not that they alone were brought into the church, for it consists of Jews also; but it was Gentiles whom it seemed meet to God to bring into relief, in contrast to the condition in which they were once, so as to make more manifest the blessing which His grace now confers on both, in Christ the Lord. "Wherefore remember, that ye being in time past Gentiles in the flesh, who are called Uncircumcision by that which is called the Circumcision in the flesh made by hands; that at that time ye were without Christ, being aliens from the commonwealth of Israel, and strangers from the covenants of promise, having no hope, and without God in the world: but now, in Christ Jesus, ye who sometimes were far off are made nigh by the blood of Christ. For he is our peace, who hath made both one."

There we have another fact, not only that they are made nigh to God but both made *one*—Jew and Gentile that now believe made one body, as is explained more fully afterwards, the middle wall of partition broken down, the enmity abolished in His flesh, "even the law of commandments contained in ordinances, for to make in himself of twain one new man". It is not merely a new life, but Christ and the church form one new man, a condition of things that had never before existed—"one new man, so making peace; and that he might reconcile both unto God in one body by the cross, having slain the enmity thereby: and came and preached peace to you which were afar off, and to them that were nigh." Thus the Gentiles had been dispensationally afar off, the Jews were comparatively nigh; but now they were taken completely out of their old condition. It is not, you will observe, that the Gentiles who believed are raised up to the level of the privileges which the Jews used to possess, but that there is now "one new man", wherein is neither Jew nor Gentile. Both, consequently, quit their previous states for a new and most blessed position of oneness in Christ, which had never existed before save in the counsels of God.

Here then is the church, the body of Christ; this is what God is working out. He is not only saving souls, He is gathering; not only is He gathering into one, but He makes the believing Jew and Gentile, while they are on earth, though previously by His own command the most separate, now to be one new man in Christ, even His one body.

There is another truth connected with the church, revealed at the end of the chapter, which I merely notice by the way. Not only is there a body formed—one body in Christ, but there is a building upon earth, in which God dwells. Although it is not my business to-night to take up the subject of the dwelling or habitation of God, yet I cannot deny myself the joy of saying a few passing words on this wonderful place which God has given to His church.

And first of all it is to be noticed, in the Old Testament there was no such thing as a building or dwelling of God, until there was a type of redemption. No matter what might be His mercy or condescension to those He loved, He could not *dwell* with man until there was a basis of blood-shedding, by which He could righteously abide with him. Hence, all through the book of Genesis, for instance, God does not dwell with men; nay, He never speaks of it or promises it. But the moment the blood of the passover is shed, and you have Israel passing through the Red Sea—the combined types of redemption (one answering to the blood of Christ, the other to the death and resurrection of Christ, in which a complete redemption is set forth in figure)—immediately you hear of God having a habitation: God could now dwell in the midst of His people. It is not because the people were better: who could imagine that? Look at Israel at the Red Sea; what were they to be compared with Abraham or Isaac or even Jacob? Yet He who only visited the fathers can now dwell among the children, and put this word into their lips, "I will prepare him a habitation." How comes this? Ah, beloved friends, how little any of us estimate the mighty change and the wondrous effect of redemption? It is not a question of comparing men, or their faith, or their faithfulness. God's estimate of redemption is the point; and He shows that if there be only a type of redemption, He can come down typically, He can then dwell in the midst of His people. I admit this was only a preparatory thing. There was a visible token of it, suited of course to an earthly people; but still the great distinct fact is engraved on Israel's history, as the very centre of their blessing, that God Himself deigned then to dwell in their midst (Exodus 15:2, 13, 17; 29:43-46).

The same thing is found here far more blessedly for the church on earth. On earth—and mark, not *before* the cross but *since*—God is pleased to make His people to be His habitation. He came down in the person of Christ, but Christ abode alone as far as the dwelling-place of God was concerned. "Destroy this temple": He was the only true temple. But when He died and rose, what then? Redemption was accomplished; and now God could descend holily, righteously, suitably to His own character, and could dwell in His people. It is not because the New Testament saints are more worthy in themselves than those of old. He that knows himself and redemption knows that such an idea is a fallacy and a falsehood; he knows that human nature is good for nothing as before God; he knows that, in His presence, there is no question of flesh, or what flesh can glory in, "but he that glorieth, let him glory in the Lord". But this is not all; not only is there a Lord to glory in, but now we have actual redemption in Christ through His blood. How does God estimate the precious blood of His Son? What does He feel about those on whom that blood is put by faith—those who are washed in it? Does He not as it were say, "I can come now and take my place in their midst"? This is indeed one of the precious characteristics of the church. It especially is even now the habitation of God. In virtue of this it is that the church is called the "house of God", and His "temple", in different parts of Scripture. But I must not dwell longer on this, because my subject is "the body".

We find, then, in Ephesians 4, that the Spirit of God presses this exhortation, "Endeavouring to keep the unity of the Spirit in the bond of peace." Next, He explains, "There is one body and one Spirit, even as ye are called in one hope of your calling; one Lord, one faith, one baptism; one God and Father of all, who is above all, and through all, and in you all."

Will it be imagined that this grand truth of the "one body" does not affect the judgment and conduct of the Christian as well as his affections? We have been brought, I will suppose, to the knowledge of Christ; we have found in Him the Son of God, the Saviour; we rest on Him as our peace before God; we call on Him as our Lord. But have I no relationship with others on earth? Am I left here simply and solitarily to look up to God? Have I to thread my way through the mazes of this world, only using the word of God with prayer? Let me ask, What are my relationships? Am I only a child of God with other children of His here and there? What am I to feel, as I look round upon those that name the excellent name—that call upon the Lord Jesus Christ, both mine and theirs? The ONE BODY is the answer. God it is who forms it for the glory of Christ: it is united to

Him. "We are members", as it is said, "of his body, of his flesh, and of his bones". It is not for you, it is not for me, to define, even in our natural relationships, our brothers and our sisters. Thank God, we are not asked: God does it; He gives what suits Him, even if it be only in the domain of earth and flesh. He does not give us what we might choose: we know our folly in this respect, He assigns each man a place—puts the high and the low according to His own wisdom. And in that which He is doing for His beloved Son, has He less to do or less to teach us? Is God's will of less moment there than in the mere outward world? Nay, my brethren, nay: even moral men dispute not the will of God as to natural relationships. We know what human lust may do—how it may break through every line of demarcation; but still after all poor man finds even for himself, without thinking of God, the need and the value of owning the relationships which have been established in nature here below. Now, is it not a most solemn thought, and is it not a fact which ought to shame every Christian heart, that in the church which is so near to God, in that which is the fruit of His own perfect love, in that which He is creating for the everlasting glory of His beloved Son, what God orders, what God wills, what pleases God, is regarded as of infinitely less account to Christians than even their natural relationships to each other? Is it or is it not the fact? Is it or is it not a grievous sin?

How do you account for this? Whence the terrible triumph of the enemy? Why is it that there is such darkness over the whole subject of the "one body" now? Is it because God has not revealed His mind? What can be plainer in Scripture? Only a portion of the proofs has been produced from a small portion of God's word; but what can be clearer than that, founded upon the cross of

Christ, a new condition has been introduced and established of God? that He is now calling out the Jews and Gentiles who believe, and forming them into "one body"?—that, as He owns no other body than Christ's, so this is His will about us, and our obligation to Him, even as it is the evident and only meaning of His word that speaks of His church? How is it, then, that such a truth escapes the thoughts of man—that you may search in vain to find it in writings new or old—that we have, some of us, long lived as Christians, and many of us once churchmen and dissenters so called, yet all utterly ignorant of its character? But if so patent, and with such a fulness of truth about it in God's word, how comes it to have been a forgotten thing among His children?

It is not because there has not been sincerity—"godly sincerity" if you will—among Christians. But whatever is near to God, whatever is the present operation of God, is always that against which Satan sets himself with all his might and subtlety. And this, because it is bound up with Christ, because it is the special actual will of God for His people. Therefore Satan seeks to thwart and mar. He does not now try so much to darken other truths, but he takes up that which most nearly concerns the glory of Christ as now displayed; whatever that may be at any given time, there is the battle-field, there the arena, where no means are untried to blind and hinder God's children from understanding and doing the will of their God and Father. When God is gathering out His church, then is the enemy's season of active unceasing effort, to oppose, confound, and obscure all the truths connected with it.

Besides, there is another question. How comes it that Satan finds it possible to succeed in the face of such evidence as the New Testament affords? Alas! the reason of this, too—the moral reason—is evident. The children of God may be the more readily deceived, because the doctrine of the church, the body of Christ, brings God too close to us—sets His grace too richly before our souls—makes us feel (if our souls believe, bow, and enter into it) the vanity of all things here. Alas! our hearts shrink from the feeling. We naturally love ease; we like position in this world; we are fond of a little reputation, it may not be perhaps in the vulgar world, but in the so-called church—something, at any rate, for self, something outside the portion of Christ and the cross. The body is only for the Head, for the glory of God, that the Son of God may be glorified thereby. Man in nature disappears; his glory wanes and vanishes; his will is judged as sin. We do not like a doctrine and practice so peremptory, and withal so heavenly. Men like to do something, and to be somebody. Man has in himself, whenever this is allowed, that which exposes him to the power of sin, to the malice and wiles of Satan; and hence it is, that this great truth was no sooner revealed than it began to fade. There is no testimony to it whatever in the early fathers, and of course a position more and more distant and antagonistic as you descend. Take up any writings you please:—Papists and Protestants, Episcopalians, Presbyterians, Lutherans, Calvinists, Arminians—all ignore it. It is not that you will not find enough truth asserted and preached for souls to be saved by; but the bare salvation of souls is not the whole truth, nor that part of the truth which reveals the church of God. Were not souls saved before Christ? Was not salvation of the Jews? Were there not faithful souls before God had a people upon earth? Was it not so from the very beginning, before the flood and after it? Most clearly and certainly.

But there comes in another thing which was not true before, which God had not revealed or established till the rejection of the Messiah, and for which He had reserved the sending of the Holy Ghost from heaven. Now in the cross of Christ God has laid a foundation for this new work, and is gathering together out of Jews and Gentiles His assembly, made in Christ one new man. Man likes to be of importance to himself, and in this world. Just in proportion as he allows this, he falls a prey to the working of the enemy; and the more easily does he deceive himself, because up to the cross of Christ there was room left for man more or less. His total ruin, his enmity to God, his hatred of grace in the revealed person of the Son, were never brought out in their fulness until then. Till then God was not, could not, be known as He now is. But the only-begotten Son declared Him, and this in respect both of sin and of His righteousness—a new kind of righteousness, which, by all means and on every side, clears and blesses the guiltiest who now believes in Jesus.

Now, if there is to be a heart growing up into the revelation which God has made of Himself in Christ according to His grace towards the Church, the one body of Christ, there must be the judgment of nature, root and branch—the judgment of the world in which man arrogates some place to himself. The church of God is based on the proved ruin of man, and is for the glory of God in His Son, as maintained by the Holy Ghost. Now, this will show the immensely important place of this truth as a matter for the soul both in communion and in conduct. Away with what does not touch upon practice and the soul's relationship to God! But the fact is, that so far from the truth of the church leaving out heart and conscience, intercourse with God, worship and service, there is nothing which brings them out so much, and binds them so fast together, save only the truth of Christ's own person; there is nothing more commanding, comprehensive, and penetrating for the walk or conversation of a Christian man.

Take, for instance, all the difficulties men gather from the Old Testament: on what are they founded? I speak now of the legitimate difficulties—at any rate what seem to be legitimate and authoritative to the mind of an uninstructed believer. What, after all, is their gist? Reasoning founded upon Old Testament precept or practice. But is the analogy just? How can we reason in an absolute way, if there be this "one new man"?—if the church is a novel special thing which did not even exist then? It is evident that conduct (for instance, found in a David or a Solomon—in an Abraham, or an Isaac, or a Jacob) may not apply now, but, on the contrary, be out of harmony with the ways God looks for in His church. I am not speaking of those moral landmarks which always condemn falsehood, corruption, or violence: no Christian is supposed to produce the sin of any of these men to justify his own evil. I speak of what was right and according to the will of God as then revealed. The moment the doctrine of the Church, the body of Christ, is seen, all such reasonings and difficulties have no more a place. God has now His Son in His presence as the risen man. There could not be such a thing as the body of Christ till Christ was there, not only as the Son, but as man, the Head of the body; Christ could not be there as man till the work of redemption was accomplished. Of old He had the title of the Son of man given, looking onward to His assumption of humanity, when He who was God and the Son of God became a real man. But how could He take this place in Heaven? He was born a man on earth. He was not a man until He was born into the world. How take this place in heaven? Christ was not Head, still less was there the body, the church, till then. "The church, which is his body", assumes that Christ had become man, and, more than this, that He is Head, as the risen and ascended man. It is only after He died, as we know by His own figure of the corn of wheat, that He produced fruit (John 12). But more than that: not to stand upon figures only, but to take any Scripture that speaks in precise terms upon it, what do we find? Read the end of Ephesians 1: "What is the exceeding greatness of his power to us-ward who believe, according to the working of his mighty power, which he wrought in Christ *when he raised him from the dead, and set him at his own right hand in the heavenly places,* far above all principality, and power, and might, and dominion, and every name that is named, not only in this world, but also in that which is to come: and hath put all things under his feet, and *gave him, to be head over all things to the church.*" Thus He has been given to the church Head over all things; but it is after He was raised from the dead, and set at God's right hand. The risen man is Head there: even He never was head till after redemption. He took His place there and thus.

What is the consequence of that, beloved friends? The body of Christ is heavenly, as the head of the church is. Man does not relish this—nay, many a Christian man finds it too high and hard. If he is a heavenly man, where is the room for the pursuits and plans and projects of literature, of science, of politics? Where are all these things that fill the mind and the appetites and the desires of men? Are they in heaven? Are warlike schemes—are courtier dreams—in heaven? You hear no doubt of the battle against the devil, who is turned out

36

of heaven, as the Lord wars by the angels of His power by-and-by. But I need not say there is no place in His body for the pride, ambition, or energy of man.

What then is the great idea of the church of God? It is the body of Christ, after He has accomplished redemption; and consequently, sin, as far as God's judging the believer, is completely gone, put away in such sort as to glorify God and justify the believer. Founded upon this, those who believe are consequently not only born of water and the Spirit, and justified from their sins by the blood of Christ, but united to Him, their blessed Head, at the right hand of God. The church of God accordingly does not consist merely of the redeemed or saints. A "Christian" means more than a "saint"—much more! I am aware there are many who think it means much less, and would count my doctrine strange; because they consider everybody in these lands a Christian, and but very few on earth a saint—perhaps none till they get to heaven. But it is to me most evident—nothing more certain—that a Christian is a saint, and a good deal more; and that good deal more is, that he is a saint after God effected redemption in the blood of Christ; that he is a saint united to Christ at God's right hand; that he is a saint who has God dwelling in him by the Spirit, for God now can dwell there. The atoning work *is* done: the blood has been shed and sprinkled. God *can* take up His abode there and *does!* How do I know it? Because God has told me so in His word. One may, alas! have poor enjoyment of it—that is another thing; but the enjoyment of the truth depends upon the measure in which our souls first rest upon it believingly: even then, unless we judge the flesh that hinders the realization of it, we cannot enjoy it either long or much if at all.

God shows then in His word, that the church is the union of believers—one with Christ, by the Holy Ghost, after He died and rose and went to heaven. The consequence is, that we must consult what God enjoins on the members of that body, if we would know how we are to walk and worship; how we are to act and feel towards the other members of Christ; and how to behave in "the house of God".

The New Testament occupies itself with these subjects, more particularly the epistles of St. Paul. It could not be formally or definitely in the gospels, because they are devoted for the most part to a living Christ, closing with the facts of His death, resurrection, and ascension. You may find there preparations for the new work and testimony—not a few intimations of what was going to be done; but all show that the building of the church was not yet begun. In the epistles, on the other hand, we have revelations altogether founded upon the great fact that the building was going on, the body was being formed. And mark another thing, which I hope to develop on the next occasion I address you, namely, that along with the body of Christ goes the presence of the Holy Ghost sent down from heaven. It is only just referred to here to show the connexion: we shall find its importance afterwards. Those who have not examined fully the testimony of Scripture will feel the weight and value of the instruction there furnished, when that point comes more at length before us. But this at least is plain, that though it is a new work, entirely distinct from all that God had wrought before, there are great moral principles, as already hinted, which always abide. In every part of Scripture, in that which speaks of the times before the law, or during the law, as well as now under the gospel, God is the righteous, holy, almighty, faithful

One, a God of longsuffering, and goodness, and truth: all this remains. Even here the difference is, that all these attributes of God shine out more gloriously, and, in consequence, deepen the revelation of God, in addition to other new ways and workings of grace which were not and could not be expressed before. What an accession of light when Christ, the true light, shone! What an infinite display of God Himself in His person! And what shall we say of the cross and death, resurrection and glorification of Jesus as the manifestation of God?

Hence, in this new man, all the moral glory of God of course abides; but now, in presence of that infinitely fuller manifestation, and the accomplishment of eternal redemption, is there to be no answer in the thoughts and hearts and ways of His children to what the God and Father of Christ is doing? If, for instance, God calls a person into the place of a servant, there are certain responsibilities that attach to a servant. But suppose these servants turn out thoroughly unfaithful and end in rebellion, and God says, "I will have no more of this; I will create a family and adopt children to Myself; I will bring people, according to My sovereign pleasure, out of the old condition into this new place." What then? It is evident that to go back to what was true of the servants might be a most misleading guide when it became a question of the children; and, in point of fact, it is and must be so. On that mistaken ground Christians meddle with the world, occupying themselves with those things that please the flesh and give importance to man. In contrast with it, God has given us the glorious truth that He has, as it were, but one man (the first Adam being done with, and pronounced to be ruined, and dead, and buried in the grave of Christ). We Christians belong to the second Man, the Lord from heaven (1 Corinthians 15). There is "one new man", not only in contrast with old distinctions, but as uniting all, Jewish or Gentile saints, in one body—His body; for that is the way in which it is presented in Ephesians 2.

The consequence is, that we need, and God gives us, a new revelation; He furnishes fresh instructions which had no place before. Supposing you had the New Testament in Old Testament times, what would have been (I will not say the worth, but) the effect of it then? Perplexing beyond measure! A Jew would not have known what to do with it. He might have been struck with the wisdom, beauty, holiness, and love of it all; but how to act upon it and reconcile it with the law given by Moses, it would not have been possible for him to know. He would have been commanded by the Old Testament to keep wholly apart from the Gentiles; he would have been told by the New Testament that they formed one body, and that they were all one in Christ—that both had access by one Spirit unto the Father. He could not have put these things together; and no wonder: they were not meant to be together. They belong to distinct times and to totally different states. The confusion of the two is one way in which Satan has triumphed in the professing church. Alas! it was not otherwise under God's dealings with the Jews. While He was standing by His law, they were breaking it; while He was holding up the unity of the Godhead, they were set upon idols and going after the gods of the nations. They were utterly unfaithful to their testimony; but I am persuaded that a Jew, dark as he was and little versed in the mind of God, would have perceived that the instructions of the New Testament were irreconcilable with his calling. But God never gave it thus. When the work of atonement was finished on the cross, God brought out these new revelations by degrees. Why? Because there was a new state of things—"one new man"—that did not exist before. Consequently, a new word of God was given, suited to bring out the due relationship of Christians to one another, and the working of God in the Church, the body of Christ.

Let me notice briefly, before I close, the practical effect—"endeavouring to keep the unity of the Spirit in the bond of peace". What interest this has, if really applicable in the face of our divisions! Consider for a moment the case of a Christian; he is awakened, finds peace, but questions what he is to do. How truly it has been the fact that many of us have been perplexed in such circumstances! We may have known very little of the word of God; but still we found difficulties in reconciling that word with what we saw around us—especially such a word as this, "endeavouring to keep the unity of the Spirit". But it is really a plain and humble path. I have nothing to do with making the unity; I have not to set up something, or join what others make. What then? I am to be diligent in keeping the unity of the Spirit. In other words, God the Holy Ghost has made a unity; and the business of the believer is to observe that unity—to keep it. What an amazing relief for a humble soul, that feels his liability to mistake, in danger of being either too lax on the one hand, or too narrow on the other!

What is the unity of the Spirit? Where does it begin and end? What is its nature and character? Scripture tells us that He has established a unity among men, yet apart from and above them. What is it? The answer is, It is in the church, which God has made the body of Christ. What a comfort it is for a believer that he has simply to judge by the word of God where the unity of the Spirit is! But how? I come to a place, and I am at a loss to know where to turn. Where shall I find the unity of the Spirit of God? How do I know it? God has left landmarks; He has given clear distinct light in His word. I search and see that He is gathering together the children of God into one; He gathers them unto the name of Christ, assuring them that where they are thus, He is in their midst. I never get the key to any spiritual difficulty without Christ. Do I merely look for the unity of Christians? It is a delusion and a danger without Christ. Christians—where shall I *not* find them? In what pit of error may I not discover some stray child of God? If I go in quest of the children of God, I may easily see them in this form of worldliness or in that; I may know them unattached here, close and bigotted there; I may find them gathered together according to human rules, and for entirely minor objects; I may hear them setting up the names of men, certain special doctrines, favourite views, as their centres of union. Is *this* the unity of the Spirit? What then is His unity, and how is it to be kept? It is that which He forms for the glory of Christ.

Christians of course are those that compose the unity; yet keeping it consists not in the bare fact that they are Christians, but that they are gathered unto Christ—gathered not to His bodily presence, but unto His name, now that He is in heaven; none the less, however, for that, but the more counting on His presence with them, though unseen, faithful to His own word. If I isolate myself where I may thus meet, I am indifferent to that which was an object of the death of Christ (John 11:52), and I am setting at nought the unity of the Spirit; if I value the one and am diligent to keep the other, I shall meet on that ground and on none other. Many members of Christ no doubt are elsewhere now, who ought to be there, as truly as any that are gathered to that name; but am I who know my Master's will to hold aloof, because others see it not, or are faithless if they do? Am I to say His will cannot be done?

Therein lies part of the ruin of Christendom; there is the painful fact, that what Christ died for Satan has set himself to oppose, and has succeeded in it. Wonder not; for everything that God undertakes is first of all put into man's hand, who is responsible to use it for Him. Alas! there is but one issue—the utter failure of man; and there will be no reversal of the tale till Jesus comes again. Nay, even then will be another trial of man—to show whether he uses the coming and kingdom of Jesus for God's glory; and the end of the millennium will prove that, as it was before, so it will be then. Nevertheless, faith overcomes at all times. See that you hold the truth fast. Let none cheat you out of the blessing which God has given, and calls you to enjoy. Founded on the cross, united by the Spirit to Christ, waiting for His return, the church is the precious fruit of God's grace.

After His people departed from the power and even let slip the bare form of this great truth, He has brought it before them anew. I cannot doubt that its recovery, in any measure, is vouchsafed of God in view of the Lord's speedy coming: else how do you account for it that God has been pleased to recall the bride to put herself, as it were, in readiness for the Bridegroom, signally bringing out again that mass of heavenly testimony which had been despised, deserted, and forgotten? Happy are they who not only bow and receive the grace of God in it but keep the treasure faithfully! "Behold, I come quickly; hold that fast which thou hast, that no man take thy crown." Be assured, brethren, that we are in the same danger as men ever were in of letting slip that which God has given us; and that every engine which Satan can devise to drag us away—taking advantage of carelessness, difficulties, trials, or anything that can tax us to the utmost—will all be put in force, because he hates not only us but Christ and His truth.

But as the Lord has been pleased to raise up again a testimony to His person, work, and heavenly glory, so I pray and beseech you, especially the younger of my brethren and sisters who are here—all who may not have felt its force and preciousness—more particularly you who have been trained from your earliest perceptions of truth, brought in, as it were, rather than out, at comparatively little cost, and who have not known (as some others) the wrenching of many a tie, with a deep disciplinary work in the heart, realizing gradually the true condition of Christendom;—I call upon you all to beware lest Satan should, in any insidious way, lead you from the only solid divine rock in the midst of the rising surges of apostasy. Fully do I admit, that all who are brought into this glorious place, the body of Christ, ought to walk and carry themselves in a way suitable to such a position. It is a deep shame where there is no devotedness beyond what existed before this further measure of truth dawned on our souls; not only shame to us, but a serious hindrance to the truth, and a reproach upon the grace of God that revealed it and brought our souls into it, that after all there should be such an unworthy manifestation of its power. But how are we to deal with this? Are we therefore to slight or doubt the truth? Are we because of our unfaithfulness, to put aside the plain word of God that condemns us for a lower ground on which we can rest more consistently and comfortably? Are we to yield to that which the fleshly mind has often sought and fallen into—to set up other centres than Christ, other ministry than that of the Spirit? Are we to abandon the only place and principle which the New Testament allows for the members of Christ's body, on the unbelieving plea that, as to walking according to this heavenly light, it is a thing impracticable in such a world as this? There are beyond question difficulties and perils neither few nor small in maintaining it. There is constant need of self-denial most surely, if it is to be walked in with God.

But how are we to judge, if not by the word of God? Are we prepared to surrender His word as our only standard of judgment? Now, while that word of course condemns deeply the shortcomings of those who are thus privileged of God—not only brought into the unity of the Spirit, as all saints are, but brought into the conscious knowledge and faith of it; while the failure of such is in a certain sense more inexcusable than that of any others, yet at least such are justifying God and His word and Spirit against themselves in a humbling way. Taking our stand upon this, that no one should glory save in the Lord, we shall find (and painfully too) that we are brought into this place to learn our faults as we never knew them—the shortcomings of others as we never suspected them. We may be astonished at the manifold failures, trials, hairbreadth escapes, and deep occasions of shame; but how come these to be so seen and felt? Because it is not the ground of the church? Nay! but because it is. And one of the most comforting things to our faith in that which naturally might perplex is, that we learn the present and permanent value of the Scriptures as we never proved it before. Take all the ways of God in discipline: they did not apply while we were mixed up with the world-church; but how precious, profitable, and indispensably needed when we endeavour to keep the Spirit's unity! Take again all the warnings about the world: we hardly knew what it was. Is it not with Christians a constant question what the world is; or is not the answer that they give us the proof of an unsuspected blinding influence? They have something or other which they avoid doing, and this they call "the world". But the moment we see the body of Christ, the world acquires a plain meaning: if we realize what it is to be among those "within", those "without" are no longer a vague uncertain question.

Let us not fear then to quit all for the honour of God in this world; let us look to Him for grace that we may bear all rather than abandon it. There may be only two or three; but yet if they contemplate the body of Christ, shutting out none save according to His will, not for any feelings of their own, it is the only thing that is or ever was divinely large in this selfish world, as far as men are concerned. I do not mean that any who blaspheme Christ, or who make light of blasphemers in their deeds, if not in their words, should be sanctioned. "O my soul, come not thou into their secret; unto their assembly, mine honour, be not thou united." It is vain to argue that the Spirit's unity can make so light of Christ and His glory. I say not that individually such may not be Christ's. We know what Satan may do even with one who really loves the Lord—how he may ensnare him into denying his Master, and denying Him with oaths too; but who would contend for justifying such sin or having communion with the guilty, till it was put away?

I repeat then, if there be only two or three, and they endeavour to "keep the unity of the Spirit in the bond of peace", with them is my place as a Christian. My heart

should go out to every Christian, in whatever circumstances, whether nationalist, dissenting, or, if there be
such, in popery; my heart should go out, spite of the
error and evil—yea the rather because of these things in
intercession. But then am I to give up diligent observance of the Spirit's unity? Am I to follow and join them
in what I know to be unscriptural and sinful, because
there is a Christian or many Christians there? Surely
not! We ought to get them out with and for the Lord.
How is this to be done? Not by plunging ourselves into
the mud, but on the contrary by taking our stand res-
olutely on the rock outside of it; and there seeking grace
from God that, by the manifestation of the truth in
every man's conscience, and by holding out the light of
Christ in the word—pressing too the responsibility of
walking as Christ's body on His members, they may be
turned from the error of their way. Never deny that they
are members of the body of Christ; remind them of that
very fact and of its gravity—that they *are* members of
His body: why should they value any other body? If
members of that "one body", why not own it, and own it
always, and nothing else? If they belong to the unity of
the Spirit, why not endeavour to keep it? God is now
raising a question, not about Popery and Protestantism,
but about Christendom's denial of His church, Christ's
body. Our business is not to originate a church of the
present or future, but to cleave to the church God has
made, and consequently to confess the sin of all rivals—
to repudiate them and come out from them. Let us put
away every human invention in the things of God, and
keep ourselves from idols. The word of God at all times
calls upon His children to be subject to Himself and to
His will. Are we so doing? On the one hand, "If ye know
these things, happy are ye if ye do them"; on the other,
"To him that knoweth to do good and doeth it not, to

him it is sin". Surely, if there be one thing in which, more than another, human will is most evidently sin, it is in that place where God exalts the Lord Christ; where He has sent down the Holy Ghost that He may be a spring of power in His people's obedience.

Though this be merely an introductory lecture, and therefore I cannot be supposed to enter into all the proofs now—only laying down a kind of foundation for the subjects which we hope to pursue; yet I do trust that enough has been said to make plain, even to the least mature of those who hear me, the immense importance of their seeking from God to realise that they are not only saints but Christians, resting upon redemption, united to Christ, and responsible to act as members of His body, diligent in keeping the unity of the Spirit and none other in this world. This is a divine obligation superior to any changes in the church's state here below. It is no question of numbers, but a duty always binding, even though there were only two or three who saw the truth.

Lecture 2:
"One Spirit"

1 Corinthians 12:1-13

My task to-night is that which I am persuaded ought to be the business of every Christian man, not in word only, but in deed and in truth—to assert the rights of the Spirit of God in the church of God. I say, "to assert His rights"; for I assume here the personality of the Holy Ghost. It is needless now to give any proofs of this any more than of His Deity. These truths can be taken for granted, not as if there were not abundant proofs in the word of God, but because they are at present uncalled for. But it is another thing, beloved friends, when we speak of the rights of the Holy Ghost—His proper sovereign action in the church, flowing from His personal presence as sent down from heaven. On this subject many find difficulties and obscurities; and great ignorance exists even among the children of God, and those too who may have been greatly blessed; in and by whom the Holy Ghost may have acted powerfully for the good of souls. Unless however we know this truth from God, unless we have it as a divine certainty in our souls, it is clear that whatever grace may do in giving us practical subjection, yet there must be much lost if we do not know the special ways in which it is the will of God that the Holy Ghost, present both in the individual and in the church of God, should be honoured. On this theme—a large one for a single discourse—I propose now to enter.

Here too, as in treating of the "one body", I would show from God's word that which was always true of the Spirit, and which therefore has no special connexion with the present time, in order that we may the better discern in what God is now manifesting Himself, and how it is that Christians—for of them I speak—are apt to be mistaken as to this. A mistake here is so much the more serious a thing, as it is a question of duly recognizing a divine person. If we maintain the title of the Holy Spirit to act as He will in the church, no question is raised about His work in souls from the beginning. No person intelligently acquainted with the Scriptures doubts the fact or its importance; neither is there the least thought, wish, or motive to do so. The Holy Spirit has always been the direct agent in whatever God Himself has undertaken. If we look at creation, the Spirit had His part there. If we look again at the elders who obtained a good report through faith, no believer questions for a moment that it was only by the operation of the Holy Ghost that man believed then as now. He wrought in Abel, Enoch, Noah, and in all others whom the Scriptures testify as the line of saints. So again when God espoused His people Israel, if He wrought in any especial fashion suited to the display of His glory in their midst, it was the Spirit of God who was the energetic power behind and within. It was He that wrought, for instance, from a Moses down to a Bezaleel, from Samson up to David. When we come to the prophets, it need scarcely be said it was under the power of the Holy Ghost that holy men of God spoke; the Spirit of Christ made them to be witnesses beforehand of His sufferings, and of His glories that were to follow, little as they might themselves understand His sufferings. Thus, in those who stand for present privileges, there is no disposition whatever to obscure, but on the contrary to give the fullest value to all that the Holy Ghost has ever wrought; for in truth there never was anything of God in which He did not work.

But when we come to the New Testament, a new thing comes to view. A despised, crucified, departing Son of man was a strange sound (John 12:34). They looked for Christ to abide for ever, and to reign in glory and righteous blessing upon earth. But gradually, as man and Israel especially rejected Him, the truth—astonishing to the Jew—dawned more and more, that He, the Messiah and Son of God, was going to leave the earth. Gentiles, I am aware, think little of this; but do they therefore show superior wisdom? To the Jew it was a most startling announcement, and at first sight irreconcilable with the law and prophets. They had looked for Him, the promised One, and their hearts delighted in His presence: it was what kings and prophets had desired most earnestly. God had put the desire into their souls; but now that it was gratified in His coming, He is going to leave them, to sink down in sorrow and shame and death—the death of the cross! under man's, ay, and under God's, hand! And not merely this, but when He rose again—instead of maintaining His glory from the throne of His father David, and filling the earth with the blessedness that was foretold, and accomplishing, and more than accomplishing, all that their hearts had so fondly hoped was just about to dawn and for ever brighten this world—He was about to leave the world in its darkness; at any rate, He was about to retire again to the heavens whence He came. But if He was about to go on high, it was not as He came down; for as the Son of God He had come down to become man—"the Word was made flesh"; and now as man, risen from the dead, He was leaving the world to take His place at the right hand of God; and during His absence on high, He would send down the Holy Ghost in a way never before known. The Old Testament prepares the heart for a present Messiah, and the outpouring of the Holy Ghost as the needed appropriate meed paid to the reign of the Messiah over the earth; but the Messiah, on His death and resurrection, disappearing from the view of the world that had cast Him out, entering into a new and heavenly scene, and the Holy Ghost sent down personally in His absence to be here while He was there—all this was something wholly unexpected by the Jew. If Gentiles do not turn aside and wonder at the great sight, it is certainly not from excess of spiritual feeling or intelligence. We may find of course the wonder of stupidity; but there is such a thing as no wonder, just because there is no real thought about it. I believe this is the reason why, if there be on the one hand the wonder of men who are surprised, there is a lack of wonder in others because they are too engrossed in earthly things to be really concerned.

Now this, next to Christ, is the central truth of the New Testament; but so far from its being the solid ground on which Christians are now walking, in point of fact all is reduced in their minds to a mere continuation of the influence which the Holy Ghost has always exerted. The consequence is, that all men who reject His special presence in person on earth as a consequence of redemption are driven into the most painful expedients in order to evade the plainest scriptures. I may just mention one case: it will perhaps startle some that such assertions should be made, and especially by a person of large reputation for spiritual knowledge. It will show where want of faith as to the great truth of the actual presence of the Holy Ghost in a way never experienced before lands those who oppose it systematically. In order to escape the clear intimation of a new and incomparable blessing in the shape of the Comforter, they allege that the Holy Ghost (who had always been given!) departed from the earth when the Lord was here, in order that the Lord should give Him once more on His own ascension to heaven. Thus, the time of the Saviour's presence on earth would be, not a bright and happy feast, but dearth as regarded the Spirit of God! I just name the thought, in order that you may see the excessive violence, not to say worse, to which unbelief reduces even intelligent men of God. Need I say, on the contrary, that those who surrounded the Saviour and were blessed by His teaching had all the Old Testament saints ever enjoyed, and a great deal more? The Holy Ghost had quickened their souls, like their predecessors, by giving them faith in Christ. Besides, the disciples had the Messiah's presence and the manifestation of grace and truth in Him, and all His words and ways. No doubt there was much they could not then bear, as the Lord Himself told them; but still they were as truly believers as any had ever been before them. The fact is that such reasoning is the puny effort of man to escape from the solemn truth of God.

The New Testament is most explicit. Our Lord first of all brings out the doctrine of the Spirit; and this as fully meeting the need of man to be born of the Spirit and to have the Holy Ghost, in order that he should be able to worship the Father in spirit and in truth. But more than this, He prepares the disciples for the mighty work in spreading the truth and the grace of God. The Holy Ghost was necessary for this; and accordingly we have it in [John] chapter 7—a scripture which it is impossible to escape. The Lord had put it in a figurative way, that out of the belly of him who believed should flow rivers of living water. "This spake he of the Spirit," (which should not be given to a person in order to make him believe, but) "which they that believe should receive; for the Holy Ghost was not yet [given], because that Jesus was not yet glorified." Lengthy reasoning on such a scripture would be a dishonour to the word of God. Where there is an obscurity, we may try to explain and illustrate; but where the language employed is plainer than any that could be substituted in its stead, I feel that it is due to Scripture simply to press that plain meaning.

In the later chapters of the same gospel again we have our Lord bringing out, not merely the fact that after the glorification of Jesus the Holy Ghost was to be given, as He had not been before; but, besides, we have His personal action, when *sent and come,* entered into fully and definitely. Hence in John 14 He is spoken of as the Comforter. Mark the importance of this. We may reason about the Holy Ghost being given, as if it meant no more than a spiritual power, but we cannot thus attenuate the sent Comforter. Who is He but the Holy Ghost Himself? No one can say that "Comforter" means a miracle, or a tongue, or any operation you please. Doubtless He works in all these various ways; but it is a real person who replaces the Messiah when He leaves the earth. Just read a few verses of the chapter in order that it be made still plainer: "I will pray the Father, and he shall give you another Comforter, that he may abide with you for ever."

There again we have what is most evident. Miracles have been; tongues cease; prophecies and knowledge pass away; but here we have a divine person who abides with the saints for ever—"even the Spirit of truth; whom the world cannot receive, because it seeth him not, neither knoweth him: but ye know him; for he dwelleth with you, and shall be in you." The world was bound to receive Jesus, and after an outward manner it had Him there; but here we find One who, not having become incarnate, could not in any way be brought before the eyes of the world. I admit of course that the world does not really receive Jesus in a spiritual manner any more than the Holy Ghost; but still there is a pointed reference to the manner of the Holy Ghost's presence here below, which excludes Him from all apprehension on the world's part as an object either of sight or of knowledge.

Again in John 14:26 we read, "The Comforter, which is the Holy Ghost, whom the Father will send in my name, he shall teach you all things, and bring all things to your remembrance whatsoever I have said unto you." It is not a gift or power or influence merely, but one who is really sent—a person who teaches all things and brings all the Lord's sayings to their remembrance. Then in chapter 15:26, "But when the Comforter is come". It is not merely in this case "sent" (because some might argue perhaps about the sending of an influence) but "come". "When the Comforter is come, whom I will send unto you from the Father, even the Spirit of truth [in every way guarding this most weighty theme], which proceedeth from the Father, he shall testify of me: and ye also shall bear witness, because ye have been with me from the beginning." Assuredly we have the Holy Spirit's coming presented with solemnity and distinctness. In the former chapter the *Father* sends Him in Christ's name; in this *Christ* sends Him from the Father. In the one case He is said to bring all things Christ had spoken to their remembrance; in the other He comes down from the Son, and bears witness of Him. They had been conversant with Him upon earth, and were to attest it as witnesses; also the Spirit from Him in heaven comes down, that there should be as it were these joint witnesses of the Lord Jesus Christ.

Then in the sixteenth chapter of John we have the truth still further unfolded, and, if possible, with increasing energy, as it is indeed of the deepest interest and importance. In chapter 14 the Lord had told them that they ought to rejoice because He went to the Father. He was leaving a scene of humiliation and suffering to be in the home of the Father's love and glory. Had their love been simple, had they been thinking of Him, not of themselves, they would have rejoiced because He was going to the Father. But now in chapter 16 He puts it upon other ground: "It is expedient for *you* [and not only as it were for me] that I go to the Father." What! expedient for those poor weak trembling disciples that He had watched over, in the face of all Israel who despised Him and would not be gathered to Him? Surely under His wing He had gathered those little ones, and sheltered them; yea, in the very hour of His own rejection He had turned His hand upon them. And now He must leave them. It was *expedient for them* that He should go to the Father. How could this be? There is but one answer; and it is the answer that the Lord gives. It is what in His mind made it expedient. Blessed as it was to have the Messiah, His presence (just because He was a man upon earth with a group of disciples around Him) was necessarily limited. He could not thus be as man everywhere throughout the earth. The Holy Ghost had not, like the Son, taken human nature into union with His person. But more than that, when redemption was effected, He could in the most intimate way bring into the hearts of the disciples all the value that flowed from Christ and His work—Christ exalted to heaven and estimated of God the Father there.

Thus then were the great foundations of truth laid. The Lord Jesus would not leave this world or go to the Father, until every question that God had with guilty man was settled for ever. When sin was put away by the sacrifice of Himself on the cross, when righteousness was established in Christ risen from the dead and exalted on high, it was not merely all pure grace as before, but now it became a question of God's righteousness through the work of the Saviour. The efficacy of His blood turned the scale in favour of man; for it was the man Christ Jesus who had thus glorified God about sin. No doubt He was His own beloved Son, the inestimable gift of His own grace; and man could boast nothing, for He was despised and rejected of man— hated without a cause. Still, there was the fact that God had so looked down upon earth, more especially upon the cross, to find the man who suffered all, that God Himself might be glorified. This truth changed everything. Now it became a question, so to speak, for God: what could He do for this blessed man? If He was God's Son, was this a reason why He should love or exalt Him less? He raises up from the grave the man Christ Jesus, and sets Him at His own right hand. That was not only a personal act in honour of Christ, but for believers it is the measure, in infinite grace, of acceptance which is now theirs in virtue of Him. All heaven was filled with wonder and praise at the sight of man, made a little lower than the angels, taken up in the person of Christ far above all principalities and powers to sit on the throne of God. Yea God Himself from that moment has made it His business and delight to show His value for the man who, in the face of sin and death and Satan and divine judgment, retrieved all His character, and brought glory to His name in delivering, by suffering for, the guilty to the uttermost. Before this man had been the constant public agent in dishonouring God. Never was God so slighted, insulted, provoked by any of His creatures as by man. Satan, when he left his first estate, once and for ever forfeited his place. There might still be a more terrible judgment awaiting him; but there was no mercy—no beam of hope pierced through the darkness into which sin plunged a fallen angel. But now, after man had preferred darkness to light, after his manifold course of rebellion against God was run, the tide was turned in the death of Christ, and God was placed by His work under an obligation, so to say, to man to bless him by faith through and in Christ the Lord.

Hence that expression of which St. Paul is so full "the righteousness of God". If man was more than ever proved to be lost, God now had a debt to pay. As a part of His discharge of it, He sets the Lord Jesus as man at His own right hand; He justifies freely and fully every believer; and He sends down the Holy Ghost in order that He might be the divine link between that blessed Man in glory and those who believed in Him, even such as had trembled at the thought of His departure. What a change there is now! Not only was there spiritual intelligence now, but power also. Peter, who had denied the Lord, could now stand boldly forward and say, "But *ye denied* the Holy One and the Just." They were all dumb. *His* denial was completely gone, and I might venture to say with more glory to the Lord than if he had never uttered it. A positive strength and triumph glowed in his soul, a knowledge not only of his own weakness and worthlessness, but of God, of resurrection, and of His grace—a sense of what Christ was for him that was beyond all he had ever known before. I do not say beyond grace, unless Peter had done what he did; but surely there was immense force in his words. They knew well what he had done, publicly done, in the high priest's hall, and before people ready enough to see the faults of a disciple. Yet he who repeatedly and recently denied his Lord was, through abundance of grace, so full of courage as to stand forth and confront and tell them that it was *they* that "denied the Holy One and the Just". His conscience was purged; he had no more conscience of sins (Hebrews 10): all was blotted out that could be against him before God. Yea he was justified from all things.

This was merely one fruit, precious as it was; and out of what did it grow? Peter had been a believer before, and was already born anew: what then was its spring? It was part of the result of the great salvation made good in the power of the Spirit of God come down from heaven, and thus working in Peter. No doubt there was previous moral exercise, deep penitence for his sins, and the restoration of his soul; but more than all this followed,— the gift and positive power of the Spirit. It is here, though not here only, that the church shows its weakness through unbelief. To the believer it is not a mere negative question now, but one of real present power; as was said of Timothy—who needed to be reminded of the fact—that it was not a spirit of fear he had received, but of power and of love and of a sound mind.

But now we must return to the great truth: the Lord Jesus, in John 14, 15, 16 shows what was to replace His personal presence upon earth—a real divine Paraclete— He whom we call the third person in the Trinity. I do not however admire the expression "second" or "third" person; and for this reason, that it tends to bring in a subordination in the Godhead where scripture does not. You cannot have a secondary God. You may bring human reasonings into the subject, and talk about a son, and his subjection to his father; but therein is the very thing which is so dangerous, and of which, to my mind, the devil has taken great advantage. The scripture shows that the Father is God, the Son is God, the Holy Ghost is God; that they are one and all equally Jehovah. Subordination in respect of Deity is only a means of undermining the proper Godhead of the Son and the Spirit. The notion of subordination is true only when we look at the place of manhood the Son deigned to take, or at the office the blessed Holy Ghost is now filling to the glory of the Son, just as the Son served and will yet reign to the glory of God the Father.

To return, however—the Lord Jesus tells us it was expedient that He should go away;—"For if I go not away, the Comforter will not come unto you; but if I depart, I will send him unto you. And when he is come, he will reprove the world of sin, and of righteousness, and of judgment: of sin, because they believe not on me; of righteousness, because I go to my Father, and ye see me no more; of judgment, because the prince of this world is judged." Any particular notice of this scripture is not the point now, but rather the general truth. This was the twofold purpose of the Holy Ghost in coming here below. He proves that the world was under sin; that there is no righteousness here, but only in the Just One with the Father; and that as to the prince of this world, he is judged—the sentence not executed, but he judged. There was hope for the world with the Jew; but now, from the point of view in which the Lord speaks of His own going and the Holy Ghost's coming, the world is evidently lost, and the Spirit here is but its reprover. Next, this same Holy Spirit should lead the disciples into the truth, taking of the things of Christ, and glorifying Him. There is thus a double relation of the Holy Ghost—to the world, as a system outside and condemned; to the saints, whom He leads, telling them of things to come, yea, of all things pertaining to Christ and His glory. Such is the plain doctrine of the Apostle John as to the Spirit.

Thence we come to the Acts of the Apostles: is there anything there that, as a matter of fact, answers to our Lord's promises? There need not be a doubt. In chapter 1 the disciples are with the Lord, entering but very feebly into that which had filled His heart before He went away. They were still looking for the kingdom with great things for the earth and for Israel. They were not, it is true, sunk so low as the unbelieving thoughts of Gentile Christendom—*i.e.*, a millennium without Christ! the shame of those who boast so proudly in our day; but still they were not far raised above the ordinary thoughts of Jews. They did not yet enter into the precious Christian hope, and for this simple reason: the thoughts of the Christian are the thoughts of heaven. They are the communications of the Holy Ghost that suit the Father, because centring in the Son and His heavenly glory. Into that communion we are brought; and truly it is not merely with the prophets and with their blessed visions of coming glory for the earth, but "with the Father and with his Son Jesus Christ". But as for the disciples in

Acts 1 the power of entrance was not yet there, for the Holy Ghost was not personally come; and yet they had not only life at this time, but life in resurrection. The Lord had actually breathed upon them the very day He rose, and said, "Receive ye the Holy Ghost." Of course this was not the gift of the Comforter as such, the promised One that was to take the place of Christ upon earth; but rather the communication by the Holy Ghost of His own risen life. Therefore, I believe, did He breathe upon them: a clear allusion to the Lord God breathing on Adam. Of old it was the breath of natural life given to Adam. Here was One upon earth who was both Lord and God (as acknowledged by Thomas a little after), and also the risen man or last Adam, the quickening Spirit. Accordingly, He communicates this life, as life must always be communicated, by the Holy Ghost; and therefore it is said, "Receive ye the Holy Ghost." But for all that, we know from Acts 1 that the Spirit, the Comforter, was not yet come. Indeed, we ought to gather it from the simple fact, that the Lord was not yet gone. "And if I go not away, the Comforter will not come." He was seen there; and He commands them, when assembled together, that they should not depart from Jerusalem, but should wait for the promise of the Father. Whatever the blessing, then, they had received on the resurrection-day, it was not the accomplishment of the promise of the Father.

The next chapter shows us the Holy Ghost acting on earth in the absence of Christ; and this in various ways. It records that extraordinary display of divine grace in the gift of tongues, which, without removing, surmounted the confusion that man's sin and divine judgment had brought into the world in the various nations and tribes and tongues, which have subsisted since Babel to this day. Now the Spirit was going out with the news of God's wonderful works of grace to all, just as they were proving that where sin had abounded, grace much more abounded. At the same time let us not forget that new tongues, although the magnificent fruit of the Spirit's operation, are not the same thing as His presence; they were an effect and characteristic sign of a crucified but now exalted Lord, the witness of gospel grace and its universal testimony in contrast with the law, but not the same thing as the gift of the Holy Ghost Himself. This is exceedingly important, because the unbelief of some has gone so far as to think and say that if the tongues exist no more, the Holy Ghost is absent. What blindness to the Saviour's promise! What a lowering of the Spirit's presence! What denial of Christianity and the church! The truth is, that the tongues, and the other powers in which the Spirit of God was pleased then to work, were but the miraculous tokens that befitted His presence, besides inaugurating the gospel and the church. It was all a new and unprecedented state of things. When the Son was on earth, miracles followed His steps and word, as it was only meet, and the accomplishment of prophecy. Another divine person being come, was it not suitable there should be proofs of it, more especially as He took no permanent form, as the Son of God had done, so as to be visible? It was therefore the more needed that there should be palpable effects and tokens arresting the mind, and causing the heart of man to weigh what God is and is doing, not only as displayed in the Son, but as witnessed by the Holy Ghost present upon earth.

This is the cardinal truth upon which all hinges that we find in the great body of the New Testament. There was now before men a fact without precedent, altogether unknown to the world, if it did not surprise even those that had been taught by the Lord Himself to expect it— the wondrous fact that the Holy Ghost had come down in person, making His presence known by a signature of gracious power, so as to be then known and read of all men. Accordingly throughout the Acts of the Apostles you have ever and anon the testimony not only to His action and its results, but to the glorious truth that *He Himself was there*. Look at the first outbreak of the world's religious rancour in chapter 4, and His answer to it in verse 31. Take again the first public sin and scandal, where Ananias and Sapphira were charged on the spot with lying not to man but to God. But how was this proved? They had lied to the Holy Ghost who was there. The standard of judgment was that dishonoured person who was in their midst. This measure of sin, let me say, is as true individually as it is in the church. Hence, in Ephesians 4:30, it is not merely that you should not violate this or that command, but "grieve not the Holy Spirit of God, whereby ye are sealed unto the day of redemption." Let us note it well.

The more this is reflected upon, the more its immense moment will be felt by the children of God. Supposing you take the presence of one you most value and delight in, does not his or her coming affect all your ways and words just in proportion as you realize and love their presence? We might be ever so much at ease; but still, if there be one staying with us, who draws out our honour and esteem, the influence is felt deeply and at once except by a stone. Surely one does think of that which will give pleasure; one rightly fears to wound; the heart is on the alert and active, and it is a joy to do that which will gratify those we love. And so in virtue of redemption the Holy Ghost is here, because as regards each believer all is gone that was offensive to God; and the saint stands in divine righteousness before God— become this in Christ. How indeed *could* the Holy Ghost be away? He must have His part when that which was most precious to God and man was wrought. If the Father accomplished His thoughts in and by the Son, could the Holy Ghost be absent or inactive? And now God had done His greatest work—the atoning work of Christ. Where therefore the blood of the accepted sacrifice is, the Holy Ghost not only can work but must dwell. If Christ by His own blood has entered in once for all into the holies, having found an everlasting redemption, the Holy Ghost is come to abide with us for ever. All hangs on and is measured by this. Accordingly the book of the Acts is far more the acts of the Holy Ghost than of the apostles, important vessels of His power as they were, though not they only. We have seen, where it was a question of sin, He judges by His presence and acts upon this ground. We have seen that, when they were in danger of being alarmed by the threats of man, the Spirit gave cheering evidence of His mighty presence. It was not merely Peter and John, or anybody else; but the place was shaken where they were. Whose presence was this, or in whom particularly? It was the presence of the Holy Ghost, not merely in this or in that individual, but in the assembly of God. More than that, the Spirit of God in chapter 13 of the Acts takes an active place, and sends out Paul and Barnabas. "Separate me", He says, "Barnabas and Saul for the work whereunto I have called them." "So they, being sent forth by the Holy Ghost, departed." I am now referring to the case only to show that it is not a question of miracles, tongues, or powers, but of a real divine person, who was the chief agent as present in the church of God; and that this personal presence of the Spirit in man was a new thing, previously unexampled in the plan and ways of God. (Compare also Acts 8:29, 39; 15:28; 16:7; 20:23; 21:11.)

Now we come to the Epistles, passing by the scriptures which attest the Holy Ghost's presence in the individual. All-important as this is, it is not my subject, but His presence in the church. Hence we must omit the Epistle to the Romans, which takes up our individual relation towards God, and for the simple reason that there we are regarded as His children. We are brought out of the place of wrath and sin, made children of God, and if children, then heirs: the Holy Ghost gives the spirit of adoption, and fills the heart with hopes of the inheritance which is to follow. But in the Epistles to the Corinthians you have not merely the state of man and the revelation of divine righteousness, with their consequences in sinners and saints, as in Romans, but the church of God, in a grievous state of sin, shame, and disorder, but still the church of God. Accordingly the doctrine of the Holy Spirit as there dwelling is shown as in its capital seat. The portion read (1 Corinthians 12:1-13) developes His action in the church. What can be plainer? Here we have the Holy Ghost viewed as a real person present and working in gifts of outward sign, no doubt, as well as in ways of edification. But whatever might be the form of His action, the great truth was that *He* was there and at work in the many members of God's assembly. The question is, was *all this* a temporary display, or was His presence for ever the substratum of it all? Was that which we here read confined to a particular local assembly and a special epoch long past, or is there anything for us, for the church of God at large, for this time and all times? The answer cannot be doubtful, if we are subject to the word of God. Certainly our Lord had in John 14 laid down, in contrast with His own temporary absence, that the Spirit of truth was to abide with His disciples for ever.

But next the First Epistle to the Corinthians could not open without the Holy Ghost's giving it the most enlarged application. In the first verse of the first chapter we read, "Unto the church of God which is at Corinth, to them that are sanctified in Christ Jesus, called to be saints, *with all that in every place* call upon the name of Jesus Christ our Lord, both theirs and ours". This is not said in the Second Epistle: indeed I am not aware that there is anything exactly like it anywhere else in the New Testament. Are we to suppose this was a mistake? Let who will be guilty of such a speech or thought, I trust there is no soul here that would not denounce it as a sin against God. A mistake in the word of God! On the contrary it seems to me to be the special wisdom and goodness of the Spirit who foresaw the unbelief of Christendom; it was the Spirit of God who knew that this Epistle would be treated as if it were of private application, as if it belonged to a bygone time and place, and did not appertain to all that call upon the name of the Lord Jesus Christ—"both theirs and ours". This He has guarded against at the very threshold, and made such an objection to be plain fighting against the word of God. Thus it ceases to be a question of opinion. God has spoken and has written that we may believe Him; and this epistle has a purposely enlarged scope, so that unbelief as to the perpetuity of the Holy Ghost's action in the assembly, as long as He and it are here, should be treated as a sin, as a positive rejection of God's plain word. Is it not unbelief which makes null and void the Holy Ghost's personal presence in the church?

It is not at all contended that the Holy Ghost necessarily works in every way as of old, and still less in the same measure of power. In the latter part of the New Testament we do not read much about miracles—very little—less and less too as time passes on. We can understand that, in the opening of a new dealing of God, there should be, in His goodness, a wonderful working and display of these mighty powers to awaken the attention even of careless men. But, as the truth of His presence was established, and the new communications of God were gradually written, and there was thus not merely the evidence of outward tokens, but positive scripture committed to human responsibility, we can easily see that external vouchers were no longer so requisite, and that the Spirit of God (grieved, as we knew, by much found in those who professed the name of Christ) might gradually withdraw, not Himself, but the manifestation of mighty signs, and refuse to put outward ornaments upon that which dishonoured the Lord Jesus.

It is certain and evident, at least when we come to the churches of the Apocalypse, that we see or hear no more of the powers of the age to come. Not a doubt have I that there was the wisdom of God in thus ordering in view of the state of things that was fast coming in. I think we can readily discern by spiritual considerations why it would not have been suitable to the glory of God to continue those miraculous powers. Supposing, for instance, God were to work now in the way of miracle, is it not evident that in one of two ways it must be? Either He must work wherever the name of Christ is preached and known at all; and what would be the consequence of this? Miracles in Rome, miracles in Canterbury, miracles among Presbyterians, Independents, Wesleyans, Baptists, Pædo-baptists, Calvinists, Arminians,

Lutherans: Greek church and all sects and denominations in Christendom would have their miracles! There may be those who would enjoy the sight, but I envy them not. Every one here, I trust, would feel deeply the anomaly of such an outward seal on such a mass of confusion. On the other hand, supposing God were pleased to say that He could not give these tokens of His power and glory where the church was thus in disorder and rebellion, but must single out—whom shall I say? It could not be, it ought not to be: God forbid that we ourselves should desire it, as things are.

But let us for the moment imagine the Lord looking on any children of God anywhere gathered, and saying, "I see where My people are subject to My word; and where I find two or three here and there gathered unto My name, there I will work miracles." What would be the consequence? We should not know how to behave ourselves! So weak are we, so foolish, so apt to be full of ourselves, even now in the face of continual weakness, as well as hatred and contempt, that we should not be able to contain ourselves if we had these displays of divine power. Besides, what a slight to those we own to be as truly members of Christ, and as truly indwelt of the Spirit, as any of us!

I am persuaded then there is perfect grace and wisdom as to this in the ways of God. He no longer works thus. But here is the truth on which I take my stand this night: the Holy Ghost was given, not merely as a display of power in the earth, but, if I may so say, as both sign and substance of the divine value for the cross. God the Father gave the Holy Ghost as the seal of that redemption which is always unchangeably perfect and infinitely efficacious. I dare to say it, and yet I say it with all reverence, that if the Holy Ghost were now taken from the poorest and feeblest of His saints upon earth, it would not be a dishonour to him so much as to the Son of God and His atoning work. It would be virtually to say that the ruin of the church has made the blood of Christ less precious; but will God ever confirm a lie? And here is the stronghold of faith—in this we can be confident— not only that the Lord Jesus has expressed the mind and intentions of God, but that we through His grace can and ought to enter in measure into its ground, reason, character, and aim, as well as meaning.

All this we may by faith appreciate and enjoy, for He has explained it to us. Wherefore indeed is the word of God given, if it be not that we should understand His mind, feel His love, and be sure of His truth, wisdom and goodness? Hence we are aware that God, in sending the Spirit to abide always whatever may be the sorrowful condition of believers individually and collectively, did not give a mere token of approving them, but rather the only adequate pledge of His delight in the personal work of His beloved Son. The Holy Ghost, we know, descended on Christ when He was upon earth without blood, because He was always sinless, as perfect here morally as He was and is in heaven, no less absolutely holy as man than as God. It is not forgotten, of course, that He had yet to be made perfect in another sense, as becoming captain and author of salvation, and to be consecrated as heavenly priest. It is clear that there was a work to be done, and an official place of glory to be taken; but nothing ever did or could add to His moral perfectness. Hence, I repeat, He could and did receive the Holy Ghost for Himself as man without blood. But when Christ went up on high, He received of the Father the promise of the Holy Ghost. What amazing comfort, confidence, and rest should this give us! Had the Holy

Ghost been given directly to us, we might well think that, if we did not carry ourselves as we ought, there might be a revocation. We can understand a soul troubled with such a thought; but, thanks be to God, the Father gave the Holy Ghost a second time to Christ. When He went on high, He received of the Father the promise of the Holy Ghost, and shed forth that which was seen and heard at Pentecost. Thus the gift is entirely in virtue of Christ, after He had blotted out our sins and received it as a consequence. There we have the firmest and surest ground on which the perpetuity of the presence of the Holy Ghost in the saint and in the church rests before God—His love to Christ, and His estimate of Christ's work for us, not to speak of His immutable word.

And now for a few practical words on this before I have done. We shall have other applications and results of it in subsequent lectures, so that the less may be said now. If there be a divine person on earth who is now in each saint individually, and with all as the church of God, I ask, Can this be a secondary consideration? Is this a truth that can be subordinated to circumstances? Is it something that can be pushed aside for the sake of not disturbing oneself or others? Can men who so think, and speak, and act, believe in the reality of the Spirit's personal presence and present operation according to scripture? Do they know that the Holy Ghost is really in the church on earth? I am not now, of course, alluding to His divine glory whereby He fills all things, because it is always true,—as true before Christ came as it has been since, and equally true of all the persons in the Trinity. But as the Son came down from heaven and was here a man for some thirty or more years upon the earth but is actually gone, so now the Holy Ghost is come down personally to abide with and in us in such sort as was unknown before, save only in Christ. The Holy Spirit, I say, has come now to be in us personally; and just as Christ was God's only true temple, so now the church is the temple of God; for both these truths are taught in the word of God. But if this be believed, if it be received as God's truth, what can compare with it in importance as a present practical fact, as well as privilege, for the saint and for the church? Accordingly the responsibility of Christians, if we apply it to their meeting, is that their assemblies should be governed by the truth that the Holy Ghost is there.

But how does the Holy Ghost work when owned as there? This we have answered, if it were only in the scripture already read. He distributes, or divides, to every one severally as He will. Is His presence then not to be recognized? Is His working not to be respected? What do we find, if we test the present aspect of Christendom by the word of God? It is far from my desire needlessly to trouble any one, nor is it my wish to provoke controversy; but there are truths which manifestly admit of no compromise: indeed, all divine truth refuses such unworthy dealing. How, then, I would ask, is it with our souls in the feeling, in the faith, in the allegiance that we pay to this truth, so vital to the church, so essential to the right honouring of the Holy Ghost and of the Lord Himself? Do you doubt that the church of God is in disorder? Where is the serious-minded Christian that does not own it more or less? Is there a spiritual man who would maintain that the present state of the church answers to what we read in the New Testament? Am I not to feel and to humble myself before God for my own and the church's sin in this grave matter? Must I not seek to be where the Holy Ghost's presence is owned? It matters not where I have been ignorantly; I have doubtless been where there was not even the show of owning His presence and action according to the scriptures; I may have joined others in praying God to pour out again the Holy Ghost, as if He were *not* come and in the church of God. And do you call such prayer as this a scriptural recognition of His presence? What can be conceived a more decided or more evident ignoring of the truth that the Holy Ghost is here? Were it prayed that the Spirit of God might not be grieved, or that the saints might be filled with Him, it were scriptural. What would it have been for a disciple in the presence of Jesus to have asked the Father to send His Son?—to raise up the Messiah when the Messiah was actually there? Is it not the spirit of the world, which cannot receive the Spirit, because it seeth Him not, neither knoweth Him? But we know Him—at least we ought to know Him. Well, if we do know that He is here, is it a light thing whether or not we are subject to His operation in the church? It is in vain to say, "I acknowledge the truth of His presence"; so much the worse, if I am not subject to the scripture, which leaves no doubt how He acts for Christ's glory. Mere words do not suffice: God looks for faithfulness, for subjection to His word, for practical recognition of the presence of the Holy Ghost.

We come together, it may be ever so few: what do we count on? We are weak and ignorant, but we have One in our midst who knows all things, and is the source of all power. Are we content with Him? Can we confide in Him in the face of dangers and difficulties? Why is it that the church is weak? Why is it that there is such want of power and joy and peace and comfort among the children of God? Can it be wondered at? What I wonder at is rather the mercy and astonishing patience of God, blessing as He does in spite of so much unbelief. Do you really suppose that it can be an indifferent thing to God? Does He not call for my unhesitating adhesion to His will, duly owning His Spirit's presence and free action? What about your bowing down to the great present fact, that in virtue of redemption and in honour of the Lord Jesus, the Holy Ghost is here personally in the church on earth? This puts the soul to the test; indeed, it seems to me the great test for Christians. Christ, of course, abides the practical touchstone for everything and every person; but still if He is known and valued by my soul as the way, the truth, and the life, is it nothing to Him that my ways in the church of God should be on the ground He has given me—faith in the presence of the promised Holy Ghost? Is it not the truth God Himself presupposes as the very soul, the animating spring, of the church?

This does not in the slightest degree touch God's working by individuals. He sends out one to preach the gospel to the world, He raises up another to edify the children of God. This is another branch of truth; and I refer to it now only to show that, when we contend for the church's inalienable obligation to own the presence of the Holy Ghost, this does not in the least interfere with the individual action of the Spirit in ministry. Granting this in all its integrity and importance, I would put the question to the conscience of each before me, Where is there an assembly of God's saints coming together, and His Spirit left perfect liberty of action that He may employ whom He will as the vessels of His power? Are there any Christians here present who never thus find themselves in the only assembly which God's word sanctions? If there are, I can only say, Ponder that word with prayer, and ask your soul how comes this? You, a member of God's assembly, yet you never know that assembly gathered according to scripture, or the action of the Spirit proper to it! You, a member of Christ's body, yet the Holy Ghost never allowed to use you, or other members of it, to the glory of Christ and the edification of your brethren! If it be so, how comes it? Why should you go on thus?

It is granted that there are serious questions here, and many obstacles; and I am sure we ought to pray much for those that are thus perplexed and encumbered. Let me not disguise from them what it costs in this world to be true to the Lord and the unerring word of God. It is not for any one (the Lord keep us far from it!) to look lightly or coldly on those who are in this grievous trial: we may have known some of its bitterness ourselves. What do we desire for God's children? Nothing less than their deliverance, yea, of every one. Do not all saints who rest upon the redemption of Christ belong to the body? Has not God set them as it pleased Him in His church? And what are we doing? Are we gathering together to improve on the Spirit's action in the church of God? God forbid: rather is it to honour the Lord in the assurance that He is in our midst. Our only true reason, if we have a divine reason at all, for meeting together in the name of the Lord Jesus, is that it is His own will and way; it is to please Him. And if it has been done at cost, God blesses this greatly, and blesses it too to the softening of the spirit quite as much as to the exercise of faith: if it is not so, there is something wrong with our souls. Am I, then, as the centre of my church-action, cleaving to the presence of the Holy Ghost? If I am not, I have not got God's centre for mine, and am still under the dominion of tradition in some shape or another; carrying on either what my father did, or something else that suits my mind better: but where is God in all this?

You may be taunted, as we all know, with bigotry and exclusiveness. Did these censors ever weigh what either means? I call bigotry an unreasonable attachment, without solid divine warrant, to one's own particular doctrine or practice in defiance of all others. Allow me to ask, Is it bigotry to give up one's most cherished associations because of God's word, in order to do His will? Is it exclusive to abandon sects, one and all, in order to be always and only where I can meet all saints according to the word, and in dependence on the Holy Ghost, gathered unto Christ's name? I am not assuming this for any one who does not own scripture as the unchanging truth of God; but I ask you who do, are you to allow yourselves to depart from the known ground of God, no matter what may be the trial within or the temptation without you? There are often attachments of other kinds that create difficulty. Friends may ask you to go here or there for once at any rate; and it seems hard to refuse, especially as they understand not the force of a divine conviction, which they lack themselves. You invite them, perhaps, to come with you, and you decline going with them. Does it not look proud and unbrotherly? Well, it may seem singular to them, but it ought to be perfectly plain to you; it may be real humility, and love too, haughty and unkind as rash ignorance counts it.

Let us conceive a godly churchman or dissenter to put this plain question: "How is it that you, who are so free and hearty in receiving Christians in the name of Christ, will not come with me to my church or chapel?" The answer is, "On your own principles, as a Protestant

Christian, you can come here with a good conscience, where we are sure the one desire is to be subject to the Lord and His word, in the unity of His body, and in the liberty of His Spirit. You surely acknowledge it is no sin to meet as we do, according to scripture, and therefore you can meet with us. But I, for my part, am clear that it is unscriptural to desert the scriptural ground for that of dissent or Anglicanism, and therefore it is not want of love but fear of sin that keeps me from going with you, who do not pretend to be meeting on the ground of God's assembly." Surely he is a bigot or worse who would urge or expect me to join him against my positive conviction, that in so doing I should sin against God. Sin is a man doing his own will, or another's, which is not God's. If you ask me to depart from what I know to be the will of God, it would of course be sin in me to comply. It is not only a thing that is sinful in itself, but it would be most especially a sin in me, because I know, if you are ignorant, that it is infidelity to the Spirit's operation in the church.

Be not moved, then, by reproaches, any more than by fair speeches. For there is no real love, save in obeying God (1 John 5:2-3). Never swerve from what you believe to be His will. You may have come in at first little acquainted with the truth or with the solemn responsibilities it involves; perhaps it was on that slender reason that you were here converted: but how is it with you now? Have you been searching the word of God to ascertain His mind and will? Do you see the presence and action of the Holy Ghost in the assembly to be the truth of God? Is it not perfectly plain and sure that God has sent down His Spirit, and that this truth has to be owned and acted upon by you and all Christians? That truth[1] *you* cannot deny; you know very well it is of

God; you may not value it as you ought, (who does?) but this is another thing. The Lord grant that we may all value it more and increasingly.

Search the Scriptures, examine the word of God for your own souls; by this means we obtain true spiritual intelligence, but this only in obedience, and we do not want it otherwise. The intelligence that is gathered in disobedience seems to me perilous and untrustworthy; to learn the truth, step by step acting it out, is a happier and holier path, and of simpler faith too. At the same time that we value intelligence, we must remember that there is another thing yet more important—single-eyed subjection to the will of God, even if we seem to be unintelligent about much. "The fear of the Lord is the beginning of wisdom." That scripture is not out of date; and I believe such is the divine and therefore the best way, as a beginning. There is blessedness in gradually growing up into the truth of God, above all looking to Him that we walk in that which we know.

For the present, I pray the Lord that the great truths of the "one body" and "one Spirit", which have been before us, may be brought home by His own power; so that all of us who know them may be cheered and confirmed, and that those who are ignorant may be taught them of Himself.

Lecture 3:
The Assembly and Ministry

1 Corinthians 14

The two subjects which are now to come before us may seem at first sight to be rather widely separated; but in truth, far as they appear to diverge, they equally flow from Christ. They are founded both of them upon His work, as an accomplished fact; they are derived from Him in His present place of exaltation at the right hand of God; they are established for the express object of magnifying the Lord Jesus, even as they are now called in a very direct way to subserve His Lordship. And this last point is one of immense practical importance. For whatever may be the power of the Spirit in ministry, whatever may be the privileges of the assembly, still the Lordship of Christ is a truth of elementary character indeed in the mind of God, but of exceeding moment for the practical working of the Spirit of God, both in the individual members, who are His servants, and in the assembly, the body of which He is the Head. Hence we can at once see that, whatever may be the different lines that either the ministry or the assembly may take, yet they spring from a common source, and they are both intended of God to be subject to, and the means of exalting, the same Lord Jesus Christ. Now it will be my business to-night to direct attention to the testimony we have in the word of God as to both these subjects, in order to show, as far as limits permit, wherein they differ; wherein also a common principle binds them together; and above all their common end, as well as the Christian's consequent responsibility.

First of all, as to the assembly, we may be the more brief, inasmuch as we have had already the "one body" before us, as well as the "one Spirit". But I may direct you to a few scriptures which prove what I have just advanced, that the assembly of God is founded upon the accomplished work of Christ, and His exaltation to heavenly glory.

Let me premise that the church has the same meaning with the assembly; hence the word "assembly" is often used in order to avoid misunderstanding. There might be many questions raised as to the meaning of "church": it is hardly possible to create difficulties as to the word "assembly". Now the fact is that the church is the assembly. Assembly is the proper English word, rather than "church", which has become anglicized, no doubt, but it frequently conveys notions not only vague, but even opposite to different minds.

Now in the Acts of the Apostles, as compared with Matthew 16, we find clear light. The Lord, at a very critical point in His dealings with the disciples, tells Peter more particularly, but all His followers in fact, that He was going to build His assembly. "Upon this rock", says He, "I will build my church." The reason of this was that the unbelief of the Jewish people was complete, after He had given the fullest divine proof, both in miracles and signs, in accomplished prophecies, and above all in the moral power which ever hung around Him—a brighter crown of glory than anything in either miracle or prophecy. But when the Lord had, so to speak, exhausted all the means which even His goodness and wisdom could suggest in acquiescence with the will of God the Father, and the result of His patient grace was that the unbelief and scorn of the true Messiah became more and more decided, the spirit of hostility becoming more evidently deadly in its character, He brings all to issue by asking who men said that He was. The answer showed the total uncertainty of Israel; nay, rather the only certainty was that men, the best and wisest of them, humanly speaking, those that had seen most of Him, were completely wrong. He appeals then, not to some great one, but to a heart that was true—to Simon the son of Jonas; and from his lips falls that confession for which the Lord Himself pronounced him blessed—blessed because it was not of flesh and blood, with their mere weakness and opposition to God. It was the Father who was in heaven who had revealed to his soul the glorious truth, that underneath that despised form—that outcast, the Nazarene, was not only the Christ, but the Son of the living God. The Lord Jesus immediately lays holds of this confession, and, with especial reference to the latter part of it—His being not merely the Messiah or Christ, but the Son of the living God, He says, "Upon this rock I will build my church."

The Messiah, in shame and humiliation, was a stumbling-stone to Israel; but the Son of the living God confessed was the rock upon which the church is built. This was a fuller confession, and a deeper one—in all its fulness certainly new, and so treated of the Lord. Not but that, as we know, Christ was the Son of the living God from all eternity; but still for the first time He was so confessed by human lips, and by a heart taught of God the Father. The Lord Jesus, then, also for the first time, intimates that upon this confession His church was to be built; and immediately He forbids them to tell that He was the Christ, showing that it was no question now of being received and reigning as Messiah. He was to be rejected, and to suffer. Hence, on His rejection by the people, but the recognition of the higher glory of His person by the remnant represented by Peter, we have His sufferings and death at once announced. This it is which opened the door for that new work of God— the church that was to be built upon the confession of Jesus Christ, "the Son of the living God". Accordingly soon follows the Lord dying on the cross, determined to be the Son of God with power by the resurrection from the dead, then glorified, and in due time sending down the Holy Ghost from heaven. The second chapter of the Acts of the Apostles, which shows the presence of the Holy Ghost, gives us for the first time the assembly as an existing fact on earth. This is worthy of all note. The Lord in Matthew 16 had spoken of His assembly as a thing that had yet to be reared up: "Upon this rock I *will* build my church." But now in Acts 2 we find the church is in process of being built; as it is said in the end of the chapter, "the Lord added *to the church*[2] (*or*, together) daily such as should be saved."

This is a very important lesson, and full of weighty results. It proves that the church does not mean merely people that are saved, or in process of being saved. Salvation was true before the assembly. The Lord took such as should be saved, and brought them into the church. If there had been no assembly to bring them into, this would not have negatived the fact that they were "such as should be saved".

What is the meaning of "such as should be saved"? It means those in Israel destined to be saved—those Jews whom grace was looking upon and dealing with in their souls. In the approaching dissolution of the Jewish system God reserved to Himself a remnant according to the election of grace. There was always this remnant, which a time of declension and ruin served but to define. Thus, during the Lord's lifetime the disciples were the remnant, or "such as should be saved". All those that were soon to confess Jesus as Messiah by the Holy Ghost were "such as should be saved"; but there was no such thing yet as the church to add them to. Now, at the time referred to in Acts 2, the assembly or church was there to which they might be added. Coincident with the Holy Ghost's presence, we have the church; and this agrees with 1 Corinthians 12:13, where it is said that "by one Spirit are we all baptized into one body"; that is to say, the formation of the body depends upon the baptism of the Spirit. Acts 1 shows that the baptism of the Spirit had *not* yet taken place; Acts 2 shows that it *had;* and immediately the fact is apparent that the church was there as a thing actually found upon the earth, to which "such as should be saved" were being added by the Lord. That is, the Lord now had a house upon the earth. The stones were there before—living stones, but they were separate: there was no building of God in this sense here below.

Now the Lord acts upon His words, "Upon this rock I will build my church." He brings the living stones together; He builds them into one and the same house— the house of God, and this not by faith merely, but by the Holy Ghost sent down from heaven. We know that, before they thus entered the church, there were at least a hundred and twenty names who are expressly mentioned in Acts 1. They too were "such as should be saved". And I do not doubt that there were considerably more who really were brethren. Thus, in 1 Corinthians 15:6, we hear of "above five hundred brethren" who saw the Lord after His resurrection. Therefore, it is plain, there were pretty many believers in the land of Israel. The "hundred and twenty" were those who, at or after the crucifixion, lived in Jerusalem. But whatever might be the number of the brethren throughout the land, or of the names in Jerusalem, there was no such thing as "the church", the assembly of God, until the Holy Ghost was sent down to give unity—to form them into one existing corporation, whether you regard it as the house of God, or as the body of Christ. There are very important differences connected with these views of the assembly; but still it is the presence of the Holy Ghost which makes it either Christ's body or the temple of God. In 1 Corinthians it is spoken of as constituted by the Holy Ghost, present and operating in it; there also it is called the body of Christ, as we see from the scripture just referred to: "By one Spirit are we all baptized into one body."

Obviously this is extremely important, because what people think and talk about as the "invisible church"— though scripture never uses the expression—was substantially in existence before "the church"; and, in fact, this invisible state of things is what the Lord was putting an end to, when He formed the church. In Old Testament times, we all know, there was a nation which God accounted and called His people, in the midst of whom there were isolated believers, as no doubt there were other believers among the Gentiles. Thus, there was Job, for instance, in early days; and every now and then, throughout the scriptures, we have one Gentile and another who evidently manifested divine life in them, and a looking for the Redeemer, outside the limits of Israel. For all that, there was no such thing as "the church"—no gathering together of the scattered believers into one, till the death of Christ. The children of God had been scattered abroad, but then they were gathered together. Henceforth disciples in Israel were not only destined to salvation, but they were gathered into one upon the earth. This is the church. The assembly necessarily supposes a gathering of the saints into one body, separate from the rest of mankind. There was no such body before. Hence, to talk of "the church" in Jewish times, or in earlier days, is altogether a mistake. The mixture of believers with their unbelieving countrymen (*i.e.*, what is called "the invisible church") was the very thing which the Lord was concluding—not beginning— when He "added to the church daily such as should be saved".

The common error upon this subject is, that the aggregate of those that are to be saved composes the church. But the contrary appears from this scripture and many others. Up to this time "such as should be saved" were not in the church. *Now* the Lord takes and adds them day by day together, making up one assembled body. Thus, it is quite evident that "the assembly" is one thing, and the being saved is another. Of course, salvation is true of those that are in and of the church. The Lord does not leave "such as should be saved" in their old associations, but gradually builds them together into the church. But the two ideas are so totally distinct, that, all through the Old Testament, there were "such as should be saved", and yet there was no "church of God", in the sense we are now deducing from scripture. The assembly of Israel no doubt there was, and it is called the "congregation of Jehovah"—the "assembly", if you will, of Jehovah; but then that was merely the nation, the entire mass of the Jewish people. It was out of this very nation that the first nucleus of "the church" was taken; and the Holy Ghost having just come down to dwell in those that were already there, the Lord takes the others that were converted at Pentecost or afterwards, and adds them to the existing body—the church now in course of formation. Evidently, therefore, the first covenant state that was now ready to vanish away answers to what people mean when they speak of "a visible and invisible church". They would call the Jewish nation the *visible* church, and "such as should be saved" in their midst, the *invisible* church. Well, let them so speak, if they will; but all I now affirm, and wish to impress upon every one who is subject to the word of God, is that, as applied to what the New Testament calls "the church of God", this kind of thought and language is condemned by the clear and positive statements of God's word. I would not speak so strongly if scripture left the smallest shadow of doubt upon the point. But if the word of God is express, it seems to me criminal for a believer to speak doubtfully. Not only is he not doing all he should do, but he is really helping on the spirit of infidelity in the world. We owe it to our God to be firm where His word is plain; we owe it to Him to be uncompromising as well as obedient. If the word of God be thus explicit, that now for the first time we have "the church", formed by the baptism of the Holy Ghost vouchsafed to believers, and that those who were destined to salvation, "such as should be saved", were taken out of Israel and added to that assembly, then I say that the church, in the New Testament sense of the word, never did or could exist before—that it began there and then—that it consists of saved people taken out of the Jews first, and then out of the Gentiles afterwards, as we know, but both brought into one existing body upon the earth. That body is, and is called, "the church", or the assembly of God.

In due time the Lord began to extend the work. Thus, in Acts 8, we find Samaria receiving the gospel, and the Holy Ghost subsequently given to the believers. We have afterwards the Ethiopian eunuch brought to the knowledge of Christ. Then the great apostle of the Gentiles is so converted as to be the fittest witness of grace, as well as of the church—one with Christ in heaven: as indeed in Colossians 1 he styles himself not only minister of the gospel, but of the church. Only he treats of it as the body of Christ.

By the way, in passing, I would remark that Acts 9:31 has its force impaired, to say the least, in the common Greek text and English version, "Then had the churches rest", we read, "throughout all Judæa, and Galilee, and Samaria, and were edified; and walking in the fear of the Lord, and in the comfort of the Holy Ghost, were multiplied." Now the best copies and most ancient versions give "the *church*", not "the churches". I admit fully there were churches in all these districts; but there is nothing peculiar in this. But that which, I am persuaded, the Spirit of God wrote here, was "the *church*". Minds were perplexed very early indeed. The idea of the church as a subsisting united society upon the earth is easily lost sight of, particularly when we look at different districts and countries, such as Judæa, and Galilee, and Samaria. The true reading at once leads us back to the substantial unity that belonged to the church, or assembly of God, here below. There might be ever so many assemblies throughout Judæa, and Samaria, and Galilee, but it was *the church.* I admit that we often hear of the churches of Judæa, and of other countries, as Galatia for instance. No one questions the fact of many different assemblies in these different lands. But then there is another truth which has not been seen for a long while by the great mass of God's children—not only that God set up a body which did not exist before, but that wherever assemblies might be, it was all *the* assembly. Not only did He constitute the church upon earth, susceptible of daily growth, but while He extended the work, while He formed fresh assemblies in this or that district and country, it was nevertheless one and the same church wherever it might be. This scripture, rightly read, furnishes a strong proof of it; and I will now just add that the best authorities leave no doubt on my mind as to this. The word *churches* supplanted *the church* at an early day; and probably it is due to the fact that very soon the copyists, like other people, began to lose sight of the unity which God was establishing among His children upon the earth.[3] It is so much more natural to conceive merely of distinct churches, than to take in the precious truth of *the church* wherever it is found upon the face of the earth. This may have led to assimilating the true phrase to another and more familiar one, especially when the sense of unity decayed and disappeared.

From the historical account in the Acts of the Apostles, let us turn to the instruction which the rest of the New Testament affords as to the assembly. First, the Lord in Matthew 18 had laid down the spirit in personal matters that was to actuate the assembly, beginning with one of its members. He had shown there, that the legal spirit is quite out of place. He had pointed out in the most beautiful manner how He Himself was the Son of man that came "to seek and to save that which was lost"—not merely that He was the Shepherd of Israel, gathering His own people, but that He was come in quest of the lost, in the pure and simple and full grace of God. Take a case which He knew might occur in the assembly He was going to build—the case of one brother trespassing against another: what was to guide? Not law, nor nature, but grace. The righteousness of man would say: "The man that has done the wrong must come and humble himself." "No", says grace, "go you after him." "What! after the man that did me this wrong?" "Yes, it is exactly what the Lord has done." That is, the Lord puts His own grace as the pattern, and spring, and power that is to govern the individual, and of course also to be the life-breath of the assembly. Consequently we find: "If thy brother trespass against thee, go and tell him his fault between thee and him alone." He that was trespassed against becomes in grace the active party. He goes, and for what purpose? To tell his brother his fault. What a call for the painstaking and self-abnegation of love! And if his brother hear him, he has "gained his brother". What a requital, even now from the Lord! It would be indeed a sorrow to the heart that he should go farther astray. Thus it is that love, divine love, reproduces itself in those that the Lord is not ashamed to call His brethren. He calls them to be the witnesses, not of the servant by whom the law was given, but of Himself, who was full of grace and truth. Accordingly, then, grace is the energetic influence that works; but truth is not set aside for a moment. Still less can the Christian entertain that pride of heart and indifference that would say, "Well, he has acted wrongly; I am above it, and will take no notice of it." There would be in this a spirit of hard forgetfulness of Christ and His grace, as well as the world's indifference about one's brother. There is no allowance of either in our Saviour's words. Again, the legal principle, right as it is in itself, of dealing with a man as he deserves, is entirely excluded. Divine grace, as seen in the person and mission of the Saviour of the lost, works in the soul if we follow His voice. We know well how easily it might be forgotten, and how the heart might reason: "Because he is my brother, he is the less excusable—he ought to know better." There is truth in this: no doubt, he ought to know it; but if he does not, you may at least feel what is your place and privilege. "Go and tell him", &c. Thus the Lord does not lay down a law for the wrong-doer to find his way back, but calls the man that is in the right to go forth, not in the spirit of right, but of grace, to win him who is wrong; and if the latter hears, the former has gained his brother. If the wrong-doer refuses to hear, the thing is to be laid before others. "If he will not hear thee, take with thee one or two more, that in the mouth of two or three witnesses every word may be established." There would be as it were a combined action of grace brought to bear upon the offender's soul, that he may hold out no longer. It was bad enough to refuse one: can he refuse one or two more? Well, but if he does neglect to hear them, what then? The whole church hear and speak; all the objects and witnesses of divine grace who are in the place are intent and occupied with the trespasser. Can he reject the church? If he does, "let him be unto thee as an heathen man and a publican."

Brethren, what sentence so terrible as the sentence of grace and truth rejected? And thereby is seen the sad mistake that is often made when men talk about love, but I am afraid with little appreciation of it. There must be a love in deed and in truth from Christ Himself, to begin and go on with such a work as this. But observe, the very same delight in and submission to Christ which can carry one after a personal offender thus, not as a bare duty, but with fervent desire to win him back—the self-same spirit of faith regards him, if refractory, "as a heathen man and a publican". He may be really a converted man; but he who rejects the grace of Christ thus flowing out according to the truth, is no longer to be counted as a brother. No matter whether he is really a brother or not before God, he is rejecting the Lord, as it were, in those that represent Him on earth in His assembly. "Let him be unto thee *as* an heathen man and a publican."

This, then, is the Lord's weighty and standing lesson before the assembly came into existence; but we are not left only to these preliminary preparations of the Lord. In 1 Corinthians, and more particularly in the chapter [14] that was read, is a very full account of the way in which the Lord orders the assembly. Before calling your attention to this, let me refer first of all to chapter 12, where the subject of spiritual manifestations begins. There you find the Holy Ghost in active operation. He is at work in the various members of the assembly of God. For "there are diversities of gifts, but the same Spirit; and there are differences of administrations, but the same Lord; and there are diversities of operations, but it is the same God who worketh all in all. But the manifestation of the Spirit is given to every man to profit withal; for to one is given by the Spirit the word of wisdom; to another, the word of knowledge by the same Spirit; to another, faith, by the same Spirit; to another, the gifts of healing, by the same Spirit"—and so on. But if we have here spiritual acting in the assembly, observe that the subject opens by tests that decide between the spirits that were not of God, and the Holy Ghost. It is not a question of settling who are Christians and who are not, but of discriminating what is of the Holy Spirit from the spirits that are opposed to Him—the instruments of the enemy.

And what may these tests be? "No one speaking by the Spirit of God, says Jesus [is] accursed (or anathema); and no one can say Lord Jesus but by the Holy Spirit." Thus the Holy Spirit of God would never treat Christ as in His own person, or relationship to God, under a curse. This is a very simple and solemn test, and ought to be weighed by us—I think I may say, beloved brethren, by us especially. For in our own days a most audacious effort of the devil has been put forth. Have not men dared to assert that the Lord Jesus, in His own relationship to God as a man upon the earth, was under the curse of the broken law?—that He was under the effects, as between His soul and God, of man's distance from God? At once we discern what spirit this is. "No man speaking by the Holy Ghost calleth Jesus accursed." On the other hand, "No man can say that Jesus is the Lord, but by the Holy Ghost." When an evil spirit works, he may utter many fine things; he may appear to exalt Christ and His servants, as we see in the Gospels and in the Acts of the Apostles; but he never owns Jesus as Lord. It is the sure mark of an evil spirit to lower Jesus, by bringing Him in some way or other for Himself, under the curse. I am not speaking of His taking that place upon the cross by grace, but of His own place as man with God, apart from atonement. The pretence may be thereby to increase His sympathy towards us, or to enhance His triumph over the difficulty, and His extrication from it; but no one speaking by the Holy Ghost says Jesus is accursed. Then you have the counter-test, that those who own the Lordship of Jesus, own Him in the power of the Holy Ghost. This is no question of souls being saved, but a means of detecting what manner of spirit is active in the church. It is the scriptural touchstone for discovering those that are under the power of an evil spirit, and those that speak by the Holy Ghost. What is of the Holy Ghost really exalts Christ, and gives Him His due place as Lord. The spirit of error as surely seeks to debase His person and frustrate His work.

The Holy Spirit invariably maintains two things—the glory of Christ as to His person, and the Lordship of Christ as to His place: the one fitting for, and the other flowing from His work. Now this at once prepares the way for the important and practical truth, that the great object of the assembly of God is the recognition of Christ as Lord. We are, therefore, at once cast upon the question, Has the Lord given regulations for His assembly, or has He left us to ourselves? Have we no directing principle for the manner in which the assembly of God is to conduct itself in this world? Is the church wholly abandoned, as it were, to its spiritual instincts? Is it to be moulded by the particular age or country in which the saints may be found? I trust there is no person here who would endorse thoughts so evidently of mere nature as these. What! the Christian assembly dependent on age or country! Can those who so speculate or act really believe that the church of God is a creature of the world after all; that God has left it, like a foundling, to be one thing here and another thing there? Institutions such as these might be good or bad churches of man, but certainly one is at a loss to conceive what pretensions they can set up to be the church of God. It is of all consequence that, be it the simplest believer, his heart should understand and keep firm hold of this, so patent in scripture, that if there be one thing that is precious to God upon the earth, it is His church; that if there be one thing God is above all jealous of maintaining therein, it is the glory of Christ; and that it is not in the world yet, but in the children of God, that God Himself is now active by His Spirit, for the purpose of glorifying Christ. But, as usual in His ways, whatever is set up on the earth is always first tried here, and then it is put into Christ's hands, by whom the divine counsels are accomplished infallibly. To-day is the time of trial. When Jesus comes, there will be no further trial in this respect. The church will then enter into the due place which is reserved for it in the purpose of God. The hour of our responsibility will be over. But now is the time when the children of God are being put to the test.

Remark, moreover, that one object of the First Epistle to the Corinthians is to show that theirs was an infant church, an assembly of persons not long gathered out of the world, and hence in much practical ignorance. You see them assailed by evils that in these days would not be ordinarily a trial among the children of God. There was certainly a very low state of moral thought and feeling, and, in one case at least, such grossness of outward conduct as was not heard of even among the Gentiles. It would seem that the devil had used particular pains to take advantage of the happy liberty of these young Christians. They forgot all about the flesh, being so occupied with the power of the Spirit. They do not seem to have reflected upon their dangers. They did not walk in self-judgment. You must remember that they had few of the New Testament scriptures as yet, and that the apostle had not been long teaching them. Of course afterwards there was an amazing advantage gained through their very fall by the instruction which the Holy

Ghost gave from it to others, and, we may trust, to themselves. Yet the epistle clearly shows that the infant church at Corinth had the responsibility of the church of God. It is the only one that is expressly thus addressed—"the church of God". At that time no apostles were there, nor it would seem elders either; but I shall have an opportunity of adverting to this more fully by-and-by. There was, however, no lack of gifted people; yet remark, spiritual order is not produced by such manifestations of power, but by subjection to Christ as Lord. It is not enough to be enriched in all utterance and knowledge. Few churches had gifts more abundantly than the assembly in Corinth. It was notwithstanding a most disorderly spectacle; and the reason was, that they were exercising those powers without reference to the Lord's will and glory, and so for their own ends. They were pleasing themselves—exalting themselves. In their new-born exuberance, they were giving the loose rein to all the spiritual energy that had been bestowed upon them, and the consequence was that there was the special need of bringing them back into the ways of God.

Whatever may be the power of the Spirit by and in men on the earth, it should always be made subservient to Christ the Lord. The Corinthians did not understand this, and they are reminded of it from the very beginning of chapter 1—"Those that call upon the name of Jesus Christ our Lord, both theirs and ours." So all through the epistle you will find great emphasis laid upon His being Lord. We have it here in reference to the bestowal and character of these gifts. So again in chapter 14 we have the exercise of these gifts regulated in the assembly. The church comes together into one place; there the saints meet as the assembly of God. Did they then speak in a tongue? It was in vain to plead that the

Spirit of God undoubtedly enabled them so to speak. Again there is no question raised as to the quality of the unknown subject-matter: it might be all true, sound, and good; but the Lord proscribes what does not edify the assembly. As a general rule, in the absence of one who could interpret, the exercise of these tongues is forbidden in the assembly.

This is a most momentous matter for practice. No matter how truly a man has a power which comes from the Holy Ghost, he is *not* always to use it; more than this, he *is* bound to use it in obedience to Christ. There are certain regulations laid down to which he must submit himself. The apostle takes up prophesying particularly, because it was the highest form of acting on the conscience; as in mentioning the various gifts, he (chapter 12:28) put diversities of tongues in the lowest place. Thus he rebuked the vanity of the Corinthians; for what they made more of than anything else, the apostle reduces to the last rank. "God hath set some in the church, first apostles, secondarily prophets, thirdly teachers, after that miracles, then gifts of healings, helps, governments, diversities of tongues." Then after the most precious unfolding of love in chapter 13 (how needful in these matters!) he comes to the due exercise of gift in the assembly in chapter 14. "If therefore the whole church be come together into one place, and all speak with tongues, and there come in those that are unlearned, or unbelievers, will they not say that ye are mad? But if all prophesy, and there come in one that believeth not, or one unlearned, he is convinced of all, he is judged of all; and thus are the secrets of his heart made manifest, and so, falling down on his face, he will worship God, and report that God is in you of a truth." Observe the weight of the principle which the apostle here insists upon. God has formed the church, the assembly, as a testimony to Christ upon the earth—a testimony to His Lordship. The consequence is, whatever would give a false, or even a vainglorious testimony, whatever would prompt men to say "Ye are mad" is forbidden, no matter how certainly the power, thus misused, itself might be of God. The gift of tongues, for instance, evidently was of the Holy Ghost and not of nature; but its use is subjected to divine regulations, as we see here. And this has a wide scope: indeed, I hold it to be the grand criterion for every Christian man to apply both for his own conduct and for judging that of others. But when we speak of judging what others do or say, need I add that it becomes us to weigh all humbly and in love, seeing well to it that we are not thinking of ourselves but of the glory of the Lord? But I do say that we are always bound to think of the glory of the Lord; and therefore, no matter under what circumstances, no matter where, we are responsible to judge in subjection to Him.

Prophesying here, evidently, does not mean predicting, as some might suppose; nor, as others say, mere preaching. There is a great deal of preaching, which is not prophesying. Indeed, it might well be affirmed that the preaching of the gospel is never, rightly considered, prophesying; for this last is that character of teaching which lays the conscience bare in the presence of God, and brings God and man thus close together, if I may venture so to put it. Therefore this is what the apostle contrasts with the exercise of a tongue. The tongue was forbidden, if there were no interpreter; and for the plain reason, that otherwise it would not edify the church. The object of all that is done there must be "unto edifying". Whatever therefore does not edify is not fit for the assembly of God, and ought not to be allowed there. It may be well meant; it may be by the Holy Ghost, as regards power; but whatever is not intelligible, and has not the character of building up the saints of God, is not fit for the assembly. These things might be very well out of the assembly; nay, it was their proper place, as a testimony to unbelievers. But they had no business in the assembly, if their exercise did not tend to the instruction, exhortation, or comfort of the assembly; and edify the assembly they could not, unless there was one who had the gift of the interpretation of tongues, and could, therefore, turn them to present account in the building up the saints of God in the grace and truth which came by Jesus Christ.

This then is the rule by which all is to be governed. "If any man speak in an unknown tongue, let it be by two, or at the most by three, and that by course; and let one interpret. But if there be no interpreter, let him keep silence in the church; and let him speak to himself and to God." But suppose you are prophets; suppose you can speak to edification in this powerful way, "let the prophets speak two or three, and let the other judge." Here the apostle takes the example of the prophets in contradistinction to the tongues; for everything the prophet said was for the express purpose of edifying. While therefore he admits them to be in the first rank of the gifts of edification, there is this other important guard asserted, that, precious and profitable as prophesying may be, no more than two or three were to speak on the same occasion. Doubtless, they were to speak one after another; they were to speak in order and by course; mutually subject, but not more than two or three. Why so? Because it would not tend to the very edification which was the great object of prophesying; it would be overdoing, being more than the saints could really profit by; and therefore there are these defined limits. Granted that prophets give the highest character of Christian instruction; but only two or three were to speak, and the others were to judge.

"If anything be revealed to another that sitteth by, let the first hold his peace." There might be then that which no longer exists, any more than speaking in a tongue; that is, revelation. This must be carefully remembered. The truth of God may be brought, in the most powerful manner, by the Holy Spirit, to bear upon the conscience, so that even now, as then, there may be the firmest conviction conveyed to an unbeliever who might come in, that God was there. I do not doubt that this is perfectly possible, and may be now at any time; and I would to God it were always! But this is a wholly distinct thing from a revelation. God may use Christian instruction of a powerful character from the written word as a testimony to His own presence among His children on earth. But revelation cannot, ought not, to be now looked for. The apostle was instructing these saints before the canon of scripture was closed. All the truth of God was not then written; and therefore it seems to me to be the fact, that, according to the order of God, there might have been a positive revelation then given, while much of the word of God remained to be written. Whereas to pretend to revelation now would be clearly an impeachment of the perfectness of scripture, and I have no doubt would soon prove to be nothing but the fraud or folly of man, and a snare of the devil. Whatever might be the power of the Spirit of God at work now, it must be by means of truth already revealed—truth already in scripture. It is not something added to that which God has given, but the mighty use, in the hand of the Spirit of God, of what is already furnished and permanently given for the church's help in passing through this world. There may be a recovery of what has been hid by unbelief from the saints; but it is there. A new truth, revealed now for the first time, is incompatible with the scripture as the complete book of God.

If we have certain things, even in this chapter that clearly refer to what was then in existence and not now, the very fair question may be asked by a simple-minded person desirous of understanding the word of God— "Why do you maintain that such a chapter as this is meant to regulate the assembly now? It is clear that you have not these tongues, and that there cannot be any revelation of a new truth. If there are such modifications, why do you contend for this chapter as God's permanent rule for His assembly?" The answer is quite simple. The Spirit of God necessarily regulated what was there before Him; but then the great aim of all the instruction is not miraculous powers nor any other transient actings, which were evidently for the special object of testimony in the early days of Christianity. None of these things forms the centre of these chapters. What does? THE PRESENCE OF THE HOLY GHOST. To this one point all grave consideration and sober arguing of the subject must come.

Have we that one and the same Spirit still? Can we count upon His presence? Do we believe that He deigns even now to act in the assembly? How many, day after day, say, "I believe in the Holy Ghost"; but do they prove their faith by their works? I would ask you, and desire to ask every saint of God, Do you believe in the real presence of the Holy Ghost as a Divine person, who is with the church, who is in the saints, who is there expressly for carrying on the assembly according to the word of the Lord, and for maintaining the Lordship of Christ there? If we have the Holy Ghost; if He be in and with the saints still; if this be a certain truth, and not dependent for proof upon a particular part of scripture where miracles and signs are spoken of, but quite as clearly laid down where these have no place whatever; if He be positively promised to abide with us for ever, then I demand, how does He act? Does unbelief dare to make the Spirit no better than a dumb idol? Allow me to put a question or two: Has the Holy Spirit abandoned the word of the Lord as His only standard for our practice as well as faith? Or is it that men bring cunningly devised reasons for avoiding subjection to that word? But is it possible that children of God can content themselves with any reasons for disobedience? Alas! it is no want of charity to speak thus. They can quote continually, "Let all things be done unto edifying"; and, "Let all things be done decently and in order". But do they ever reflect that not even the Corinthians had so violated the order of God's assembly by their unbecoming displays, as they themselves do every day by a routine of their own (fixed *or* extempore), which does not resemble the form, any more than it embodies the spirit, of the divine order? There is the very chapter they quote on the one side; there are on the other the plain positive facts of their religious practice habitually.

You have the church of God no longer on the ground of one assembly—no longer holding to such a foundation-principle as liberty for the Spirit therein to edify by whom He pleases. You have different religious associations set up, often peculiar to different countries, and in no respect answering to either the assembly or the assemblies in the word of God. If a man belonged to the church of God at Jerusalem, he belonged to the church of God at Rome. It was merely a question of locality. He was a member of the church of God, and therefore, wherever it might be, he if there belonged to the church in that place. Scripture does not recognize membership of *a* church, but of *the* church. If the church of God was in a given place, the Christian, unless put away, finds his place within it. You never find, I repeat, in scripture, anything about membership of *a* church; it is always of *the* church. This is a most significant difference, as indicating the departure of Christendom from God's word. For in our days, if you belong to this church, you do not for that very reason belong to that church. Instead of your membership in the church of God being the ground why you are a member of it everywhere, on the contrary, so great is the change, that now the fact of belonging to one church is the best possible proof that you do not belong to another. If you belong to the church of Scotland, you have no such connection with the church of England; if you are a Baptist, you do not at the same time belong to the Wesleyan society, or to any other of the Dissenting bodies. Scripture knows nothing of the kind.

Thus the revolution of Christendom is complete. A state of things entirely outside the word of God, and contrary to the word of God, has come in. Religious societies, independent of one another, have sprung up. I am not now speaking particularly of what is commonly called the Independent or Congregational system, though there the principle is carried out more antagonistically than in any other to the unity of the assembly of God as scripture presents it. But take any or every one of them; they are all more or less independent. It is so even to a large extent with the national Establishment. On the contrary, in the times of those who laid the foundation of God's assembly, he who belonged to the church at all, of course belonged to it where he lived; but if he moved or journeyed to another place, he was received according to his place in the church everywhere. There might be in some cases a doubt as to his reality; for subtlety as well as violence assailed the early Christians. Hence they carried letters of commendation, or they were visited: that is, just the principle of what is now available can be shown in scripture. Thus, in the case of Saul of Tarsus, when Barnabas heard the news of his remarkable conversion, he did not like other disciples think such a work too hard for the Lord; but, being a good man and full of the Holy Ghost, he is quite ready to believe what grace could do, and goes and finds Saul, who is thus recognized of the church in Jerusalem. So now, if a stranger comes forward, professing to be a believer in the gospel, persons in whom all can confide visit him; and thus the church upon their representation, conscientiously and heartily accepts the confessor of Christ.

But we are not confined to any one rigid canon whatever. There is divine light in the word of God for every possible exigency, and if we have not that light, we had better wait on the Lord, and see whether the precious fulness of scripture will not be rendered without doubt applicable to the difficulty, by the power of the Spirit, without our presuming to add anything like a rule to meet the case. It is not meant that there may never be perplexity, and that we may not feel our weakness and lack of wisdom. Humility, patience, and faith will ere long prove better solvents than all the appliances of human art. God has undertaken to provide for us in His word; and spiritual power consists in the bringing that word, by the Spirit, to bear practically upon every case that comes before us.

The main point on which I insist, however, is this—that, according to scripture, he who becomes a member of the church of God at all is a member of it everywhere. He might carry letters of commendation to the assembly where he went. But why? Because all through the world it was the church of God. Now I ask you, ought we to accept as God's assembly anything systematically different from the scriptural account of it? Ought we to allow another and contrary principle to rule its public services? If we do, are we really in this subject to the word of God? You may tell me of the obstacles which exist now, and that you have so many difficulties to contend with. All this is granted: only let us hold fast that here, as elsewhere, the will of God is paramount to all other considerations. If we find ourselves accrediting that which opposes scripture, our business is to cease from doing evil, and to learn to do well.

It is *not* our duty—far from it—to form a new church, but to cleave to that which is the oldest of all, and the only church that is true—the assembly of God as it is exhibited in scripture. Why do you hesitate? Are you not satisfied with the church of God? Whose church, what church do you prefer?

But you allege that times and circumstances entirely differ now; and you ask, with a sort of triumphant air, whether two or three Christians meeting here and there can be God's assembly? Undoubtedly, I reply, there is a sorrowful change; but the true question is, does God's will about His assembly change? Which is right—to accept man's change, or to go back to God's will, even though there be but two or three who meet together in submission to His word? If I am with them gathered to the Lord's name, owning the members of His body, waiting upon God to work by His word and Spirit, is not

Jesus in our midst? And what so great comfort for our souls? I hope to prove, another evening, that this is the express provision of the Lord for these last days; but however this be, all I stand to now is, that the free action of the Spirit, among the gathered members of Christ, is the one principle of the assembly of God laid down in His word. There can be no other which He sanctions. Either I am acting upon it, or I am not. If I am seeking to be faithful thus to the Lord, blessed am I, whatever my sorrow for the state of the church. If I am not, at any rate let me confess my faithlessness. The word of God leaves no doubt what His unchanging mind about His assembly is. The Holy Ghost is come for ever to guide His assembly. All that is wanted is a spirit of repentance and of faith. There are hindrances; there are ties; there must be a high price paid in this evil world for obedience to the Lord Jesus. But am I His? Do I value His love? Is He more precious to me than all else in this world? Is His yoke a burden? Is His will sweet to my soul? Then, I say, there is but one pathway. It is vain to be loud in our profession of readiness to go with the Lord to prison or to death. This He may not ask of us; but He does in effect demand of every Christian whether he is true to His own glory in the assembly of God. It is not a question of rival institutions pertaining to different countries, or to different leaders; neither is it a question of a special school of doctrine, or of a peculiar plan of discipline and government. Is old habit, is tradition, is interest in this life, to keep me back from faithfulness to that which God shows to be His will for His assembly?

If you see the will of the Lord, do not hesitate another day. Do not wait till everything is clear. It is not faith, when God calls one out, to say, first show me the land.

Put away what you know to be wrong; never go on in what is without doubt contrary to the word of God. "To him that hath shall be given." Have you renounced what you know does not agree with, but opposes the word of God? Cleave to nothing but the word. Let me ask, for example, what you did last Lord's-day. Were you found, as a Christian, where you could honestly say, "I was in my place in the assembly of God"? Did the various members of the body come together trusting to the Holy Ghost to guide them, with an open door for this or that believer, as each had received the gift, to minister the same one to another, as good stewards of God's manifold grace? or were you joining with others where the scriptural plan would have been regarded as disorderly? If the latter, the Lord grant you to see clearly that you are not within the scene of His will, and of His glory in the assembly! I say not that you are strangers to the grace of Christ, or outside the work of the Holy Spirit— far from it. I believe He blesses not only in Protestant associations, but beyond them too. Is this to be uncharitable? I believe that the Spirit of God acts, wherever He sees fit graciously to use the name of Christ, for the good of believer and unbeliever. I for one doubt not for a moment that God has used His word for the conversion and comfort of souls among Roman Catholics—ay, and Romish priests, monks, and nuns. It may have been in a scanty measure, as assuredly the opposition to the truth is enormous, and the opening seems small indeed; but yet has it been really so down to our own days, and still more largely and clearly in the past.

But enough of this. The question is not whether the Spirit of God may not cause truth to take effect in this denomination or that. The chief thing before our souls now is, are we honouring Christ according to the word of God? Are we subject to the Lord in the assembly? Are we carrying out His will as far as we know it? We may fail in doing so—surely we all do. When you are thus come together, you may find some restless, some that do not altogether what they should; you may hear individuals that had better be silent, and you may see sometimes those silent whom it would be blessed to hear. It may be that they are yielding to a morbid sense of responsibility, and fear of criticism, and many other things that hinder their utterance of what is in their hearts. All this may readily be. Nobody denies the possibility or the fact of failure. But how does this in the least degree weaken the truth of God, or the bounden duty of His children?

Let me put a case that any believer may understand. The Holy Ghost dwells in you, if you are a Christian; but are you always acting in the Spirit? No. Does not the Spirit always abide? To be sure He does. You are always the temple of God; you never can be anything else, if you are members of Christ; but you may for all that sometimes grieve the Holy Spirit. Your obligation, however, never ceases. It is just so with the Spirit in the church.

Let the assembly come together. We will suppose they are converted, and have received the Spirit of God, and really do, as an assembly, look to Him to guide. I use that expression "as an assembly", because it is not assumed that every member understands the truth about the Spirit of God. Some of them may be very ignorant. It is more or less a shame for them, but there may be such cases, and in point of fact such there are. Some saints have been attracted by spiritual instinct, who may have been trained up in dissent or nationalism, and who settle down with little progress in intelligence. These are apt to bring in the effects of the routine in which they have been brought up spiritually, so to speak; and I need not say that their experience will not help them to be always submissive to the guidance of the Spirit. Nor is this at all confined to these only; for we know what weakness may be found among those that have been inured to the truth from their infancy. Their being where they are costs them but little; they have not known any deep sense of the ruin of Christendom. Their souls have been exercised feebly. I am supposing them to be converted, but coming into the truth of the church's position rather through parental training than at the loss of all; and so there is apt to be a taking for granted, without any divine conviction, that things are all right. Need I say how desirable it is that there should be real exercised spiritual intelligence as to the working of the Holy Ghost in God's assembly?

But then, allowing these drawbacks, and all the rest that might be added, the great fact holds good, that as certainly as the Holy Ghost dwells in every Christian man, so sure it is that He dwells in the whole assembly—in the church of God. What we have to consider is, whether individually, or as an assembly, we submit to be guided by Him to the glory of Christ. Indeed I cannot but judge it to be really Antinomian in principle, where men deliberately rest in this, that to be Christians is the one great matter—that if the Lord has shown us His grace, we need not make much ado about His will or anything else. Is it, then, come to this, that the great body of God's people not only do not know, but do not care to know, His will about His assembly? Do you resent this charge? Then search and see what is your desire as to this. Is it to be subject to the Lord and His word? Can there be a more direct test for me as a

Christian, or a more evident way of proving my loyalty to my Lord, than in this very thing? If I belong to the assembly of God, ought I not to renounce everything inconsistent with the scriptural account and regulations of that assembly?

Further, let me warn you that have taken this position, that wrong principles, false doctrines, evil ways, may slip in. We know the devices of Satan; but what some of us may have said before they were thus proved, this we may repeat with increasing emphasis now, that as God's Spirit is the Spirit of truth, so is He the Spirit of holiness also. When, therefore, the assembly refuses to bow to God's word, preferring to accept evil publicly rather than judge it for Christ's sake, what is to be done in this case? First of course full testimony is to be given, and warning, private and public perhaps, and patient waiting on honest slowness and fear, in order to bring all right. But suppose all has been rejected, and the assembly in any place deliberately prefers its own ease or will to the word of God, what then? The duty of separation is even more peremptory than from the ordinary ecclesiastical institutions of Christendom; for it is a greater sin in the sight of God for those that have known the truth of God, and seemed to be acting upon it in faith, to abandon it for any reason whatever. Ought not these, then, to be parted from with yet more gravity and horror in the sight of God, than one would turn from the meetings of those who have never known the value of the Lord's name for the assembly of His saints?

At the same time, when you find an assembly—let it be small, or let it be great—come together, owning their faith in the Holy Ghost's presence, we should not be quick in laying a sin to their charge. Surely there is to be slowness in judging an assembly yet more than an individual. Are we to assume that *our* thoughts, *our* feelings, are necessarily according to God? Hence we find the all-importance of waiting upon the Lord. But still the fact remains, that if the public sin be certain and clear, and all warnings be rejected, the more the assembly takes the position of being God's assembly, the more is its departure from Him to be lamented, and one's back is to be turned upon it, because it is now at least a false profession. God looks for truth in His saints, but He looks for it also in His assembly. It is the place where He expects the manifestation of His character before men, and not only where He makes good the edification of His saints. Everywhere He holds to the glory of His Son. I admit all the difficulties from the rising up of national systems after the great Romish apostacy, from the spread of nonconformist bodies subsequently, and from more recent attempts of all kinds. But let me press upon all who hear me that we do not contend for anything of ours, whether inherited from our fathers, or an invention of our own; we do not contend for anything because it is new, nor even because it is old—had it the green age of three centuries, or the hoary hairs of fifteen hundred years. We return to the ground which it was our sin—Christendom's sin—to have left; we return to a way which we know to be absolutely good and true, because it is God's way. We take our stand upon the only divine foundation for the church. We have no confidence in ourselves, but are sure we are right and safe in commending ourselves to God and the word of His grace; and therefore we may be of good courage. If the character of our difficulties, dangers, and trials proves how we need the scripture, we learn also how scripture applies ever fresh and mighty; and thus our hearts are encouraged to cleave to God more and more.

I have dwelt so long upon the assembly, that I shall not be able to say much as to ministry to-night. But I may be brief, more particularly as we shall have the subject of Gifts and Offices before us another time. Let me just make a few plain observations as to ministry before closing.

We have seen that the church flows from Christ risen and glorified by the Holy Ghost sent down from heaven to bind together and form the assembly upon earth. This is the only assembly that God sanctions, and therefore which every member of it ought to sanction, until the Lord takes it out of this world. We have the words and workings of the Spirit of God in the assembly shown us in scripture already referred to. I come now to some general principles. And first of all, just as the church is a divine thing, so is ministry. It flows neither from the believer nor from the church, but from Christ, by the power of the Spirit.

Now this at once clears the way. The *Lord* calls, not the church; the *Lord* sends, not the saints; the *Lord* controls, not the assembly. I speak now of the ministry of the word. There are certain functionaries whom the church does or may choose: for instance, the assembly may nominate the persons it thinks fit to take care of the funds, and to distribute of its bounty. The church may employ its servants, selecting them according to its best wisdom; and the Lord owns this choice. So it was done of old, as we read in Acts 6, where the multitude chose, and the Apostles laid their hands upon those chosen to look after the tables. So it was where "the churches" (in 2 Corinthians 8) chose brethren as their messengers; and so, again, where the Philippian church made

Epaphroditus their messenger in ministering to the wants of Paul (Philippians 2).

But we never find this kind of selection where the ministry of the word is concerned. Never! On the contrary, the Lord Himself once looked upon His poor disheartened scattered people, pitied them, and told the disciples to pray that *the Lord of the harvest* would send forth labourers (Matthew 9). The very next chapter shows that *He* was the Lord of the harvest, who accordingly sends them Himself. Afterwards He prepares His disciples for the full character of the Christian ministry when He should leave them. Thus in Matthew 25 where there occurs the parable of the Lord departing to a far country, we have the same truth—the Lord giving gifts to His servants. Now this really decides the matter. For the difference between that which the word of God acknowledges, and that which is seen now-a-days, lies in this, that according to scripture the ministry of the word, in its call and in its exercise, is more truly divine than that which is now substituted for it in Christendom. Hence also its proper dignity is impaired, specially the holy independence of man, which is essential to its due exercise, and, above all, to the glory of the Lord Himself. If preachers be sent *by men,* it is an usurpation of the Lord's prerogative, and the gravest detriment to His servants who submit to it.

What is the effect of ministry exercised according to scripture? The most perfect freedom for all that is given of God for the blessing of souls. Accordingly you find the universal doctrine of the Epistles fully confirms that which the history shows in the Acts of the Apostles. But I must refer to both as briefly as may be.

In 1 Corinthians 12-14, we have already seen that it is of the essence of the church, as God's assembly, and the aim of the Spirit's presence therein, that He should have full liberty to use whom He pleases for the glory of the Lord and the blessing of all. The exhortation in 1 Peter 4:10-11, and the caution in James 3:1, suppose the same openness and its liability to abuse. This may suffice for "those within".

As to "those without", the will of the Lord is equally clear. Thus, in Acts 8 we hear of persecution falling upon the church, and they were all scattered (but the twelve), and went everywhere preaching the word. Now, I do not call this necessarily ministerial. Of course some of them were ministers of the word, others not; but all went everywhere evangelizing. But it proves that the Lord recognizes any and every Christian man in going forth and announcing the glad tidings. (Compare Acts 11:19-21.)

But when we come to detail, we find Philip in the same chapter 8 preaching freely. "But", some will say, "he was chosen of the church." He was *not* chosen to minister the word. He was chosen, on the contrary, to leave the apostles, unembarrassed by serving the tables, to the ministry of the word. It was expressly for the purpose of relieving the apostles from the secular work, that the seven men were looked out by the multitude, and duly appointed over this lower task; the call of the church was for this only. It was *the Lord* that called Philip to preach the gospel; and the Lord blessed the word, which extended to and beyond Samaria. (Compare Acts 21:8 for both.)

In Acts 9, we see a man on the highway to Damascus with a commission from the high priest to persecute the

Jewish Christians. That was the only commission Paul received from man—an authority, not to preach the Gospel, but to extinguish it, if it were possible. But the Lord, in sovereign grace, not only converted Saul of Tarsus, but sent him out, direct from Himself, a preacher, and an apostle, and a teacher of the Gentiles in faith and verity. Paul thus becomes the standing type of Christian ministry. Apart from miraculous facts, he exemplified livingly the words, "we believe, and therefore speak" (2 Corinthians 4).

We find the Lord after this introducing others into the work, more particularly Apollos, who was "an eloquent man, and mighty in the Scriptures", but so very ignorant at first, that he knew nothing beyond the baptism of John (that is, the testimony which was rendered to Christ when He was living upon the earth). But if he was thus in the dark as to the Church and the full truth of Christianity, he was a converted man. Of course, there were souls converted before the coming of Christ. It is mere ignorance that sees any difficulty in such a statement. Apollos had received by the Spirit the early testimony to the Lord, but he did not know the work of Christ. This he is taught by a good man and his wife, who helped him in the fuller understanding of the Scriptures, and he comes out mightier than ever in the truth, and there is no hint about a human inauguration before he preaches. Yet the apostle Paul writes with all respect of Apollos, putting this unordained man between himself and Peter (1 Corinthians 3). Again, he tells them, in the last chapter of this epistle, that he had asked Apollos to come, but "his will was not at all to come at this time". Does not this indicate a very different state of things from what men dream of apostolic rule, as well as from what exists now? What it does truly illustrate is the way the Lord maintained His place. An inspired apostle gives his counsel to Apollos, who does not conform. This Paul himself records without censure; and, in fact, scripture does not say which was right: it may very probably have been the great apostle, but on this point we are left entirely in the dark. In any case, the record brings out the weighty truth that *the Lord* abides the absolute Master and Director of His servants. Man likes to regulate; but the Lord, to whom we are surely bound above all, exercises the hearts of His servants, and gives them in this word a guiding principle for all time. Is it true for your soul and for mine? Are we practically servants of the Lord—of the Lord only? or are we serving a denomination as its ministers? If we are *only* nationalist or dissenting ministers, I have nothing to say; but if we are *really* ministers *of Christ,* let us beware. "No man can serve two masters": if we have been striving to serve Christ and the sect whose officials we are, which is to be held to? which to be given up?

Thus, along with the assembly of God, there is the ministry of the word, committed sovereignly to some of its members, not to all, yet assuredly for the good of all. Let the assembly respect the servants in their place, and let the servants respect the assembly in its place. None ever confound the two things without the most disastrous consequences: neither must be sacrificed. It is the place of a servant, no doubt, to preach or teach in subjection to Christ; it is the place of a servant, likewise, to counsel, guide, govern, according to his gift from the Lord. But whatever may be the servant's mind, judgment, or counsel, nothing dissolves the direct responsibility of the assembly to Christ. The same Jesus is Lord of the servant, but He is also owned as the Lord by the assembly of God.

Take the instance, again, which is shown in Acts 13. Barnabas and Saul go forth on a missionary circuit, directed by the Holy Ghost, and taking Mark with them. But Mark turns out an indifferent servant, and speedily returns to his home. They are going out again (Acts 15), but Paul insists upon going without Mark. Barnabas, who was related to Mark, did not like him set aside, and contends with Paul about it—good man as he was—and this so sharply, that it leads to a severance of these two devoted and tenderly attached servants of Christ. Then Paul chooses Silas, and they were commended by the brethren to the grace of God. The church, or the labourers, were, no doubt, convinced that Paul was in the right. Of Barnabas, nothing of the kind is said; the subject, as far as he is concerned, drops. Paul enters on a large and enlarging sphere, and Silas goes with him, supplying, as it were, the place of Barnabas. Now there we find not only an individual servant at work, but the joint action of two or more in the service of the Lord. Barnabas might be as wrong in taking Mark, as Paul was right in choosing Silas; but the principle is clear. Spiritual judgment is necessary in selecting a fellow-labourer. Forced association with one we do not believe competent or desirable, is clearly not according to the Lord's mind.

Thus, in His service, there is such a thing as association, but no bondage about it. Barnabas was free to preach the word as much as ever. There was no lack of saints, of course, to welcome Barnabas, and no want of sinners to be preached to. But Paul would not have Mark forced upon him, and chooses another; and this is an important example for us. How completely does scripture provide both for co-operation and for refusing it! The Lord Jesus keeps His due place, not only in relation to the assembly, laying down how it is to be ordered, but also in relation to ministry, showing how the work is to be carried out on earth. The word of God meets every need.

But there is another thing that is wanted for all of us. What is this? Simple faith in the Lord, in His grace, in His word. Where this is not, souls are apt to be cast down by difficulties. Then, when they see things looking other than what attracted them once, they begin to doubt everything. How different if our mind is made up for having to do with the Lord! Let us look well to it that we are subject to Him. Of course, I am not now denying moral subjection to "chief men" in the fear of the Lord; this may be a part of subjection to Him; but what we need to have settled is, that at all times, and under all circumstances, we must please the Lord. He will be with us; our circumstances may look critical and be trying enough; but we shall find infinite blessing to our souls— indeed, it is in times of trouble we prove the solidity of the blessing. Be assured that, as the Lord went through the cross to His heavenly glory, so we shall find His cross stamped upon every service; but then, it is the Lord, and it is His cross. Let our hearts, therefore, be of good cheer.

The two lines of truth here sketched—the assembly of God, and the ministry of Christ—you will find laid down in the word of God. Both flow from Christ, instead of being mere voluntary associations: as to both we lie under a responsibility which cannot be evaded. The church *is bound* to receive Christ's ministers, instead of having the *right* to choose.[4] From Christ the power comes; to Christ the servant is immediately responsible. If a man is called to serve, let him rejoice in, but bow to, the blessed truth, that he is to serve the Lord

117

Jesus Christ. The consequence of carrying it out will be, that the world will drop off; it may be even that many of his Christian friends will look cold. The ministry of Christ was never intended to work in the system of the world, any more than the assembly of God; both were meant to exalt the Lord Jesus, and to be an exercise of faith for His saints and servants. It must be so still. More than that, it was intended that in the church and the world we should feel the difficulties and sorrows, as well as joys of faith. I do not doubt the triumph in Christ; but we can count upon trial and tribulation surely in this world. We may find differences as to the world. Sometimes too in the church of God there may be fluctuations. Every one who has served Christ knows something of this. But as to Him to whom the church belongs, and whom we serve, He remains "the same yesterday, and to-day, and for ever". The question is, are we prepared to follow Him?

Lecture 4:
Worship, the Breaking of Bread, and Prayer

JOHN 4:10-24

The first and weightiest part of the subject now before us is worship. It most of all concerns us, because it most nearly touches God himself; and this, I am convinced, is the truest criterion, as well as the safest and most salutary for our souls. No doubt the breaking of bread may be included in worship, but it calls for a separate notice, as being of a complex nature and having a distinct aspect toward the saints themselves; whereas worship as such is essentially God-ward. Again it seemed due to its importance to give it a place of its own, as furnishing most impressively, and in an act which engages all hearts, that which brings before our souls the deepest and most solemn revelation of divine holiness and grace in the Lord's death, in presence of which all find their level, all recognize what they were without His precious blood, what they are now in virtue of it, and above all what He is who so died in atonement for them, that they might remember Him—yea, for ever—in thankful and adoring peace.

The scripture read to-night shows not only that worship forms a blessed, lofty, and most fruitful part of Christian life, but that the Lord Himself puts it in contrast with that which God enjoined in times that are past. As on previous occasions a consideration of God's ways of old helped us to see more distinctly the fresh revelations of God in the New Testament, so we shall find in the matter of worship.

First of all let me premise that there is a certain state of soul that is needed for worship. God looks for the worship of His children, and it is a duty in which all of them have a direct and immediate interest; yet there is a basis necessary both on God's part and on theirs, in order that there should be real proper Christian worship. So it was with regard to the one body, the assembly of God, and the gift of the Holy Ghost. If there be one domain more than another where the allowance of man's will is both a sin and a shame, it is in intruding into the worship of God. Yet is there anything more frequently done and with less conscience? Is there an act where man more exalts himself, and does greater despite to the Spirit of grace? Let none suppose that this is speaking with undue severity. Can one speak too strongly of an interference which deludes the world, defiles the Church, and destroys the moral glory of Christ? On a false foundation or rather without foundation man all the while is but actively dishonouring God, and this in the face of the brightest manifestation He has made or can make of Himself; for it is in His Son. If in truth God has so spoken and acted, then we have God fully revealed; and we must have one superior to the Son of God in order to find a brighter and fuller revelation than what we have in Christ.

This then is both the source of all our hopes and blessedness, and the basis on which Christian worship proceeds; nevertheless, though it is absolutely essential to Christian worship that there should be a perfect revelation of God in Christ, this infinite as it is does not suffice. There is a need on man's part which must be met according to divine glory. God has not failed to reveal Himself fully; He has left nothing undone; He has done nothing that is not absolutely perfect; and all this so that there need be no doubt or question about it.

There was doubtless a gradual unfolding of God's mind and will and glory: indeed I think we might say that He could not have brought out all His mind until He gave His Son. But now that the Son of God is come, we can as believers say without presumption—"He has given us an understanding, that we may know him that is true." In fact, we should be deliberately slighting or guilty disbelieving what God has given in order that He should be known, if we did not say boldly "We know." Is it not a great thing in a dark world like this to have God preparing, even for His babes, such language as "we know"? Yes, and He would have us prove the truth of these words "we know", not only as to ourselves but Himself. It is much to have a divine book in which we can, as led of the Spirit, look back on the past, forward on the future, down upon the maze of the present, and say as to all "we know". It is infinitely more and better that we can humbly and truly say, "we know Him that is true, and we are in Him that is true, even in His Son Jesus Christ" (1 John 5).

It is not a question of how far there may be intelligence developed in the child of God. There is such a thing as growth in knowledge; but along with it we must also stand up for the great blessing and fundamental truth, that every soul God has brought to Himself has an unction from the Holy One and knows all things. Now the possession of this divine capacity is far beyond any measure of difference there may be in practical development. Of course there are such differences, and there is thus room for the exercise of a spiritual mind, and the Spirit of God no doubt acts through the truth upon us that we may make progress. But then we may rest confident, as we think of the children of God, that, wherever they are, under perhaps the most untoward circumstances, God has given them a new nature, and this a nature capable by the Spirit of understanding and appreciating and enjoying Himself. All the time here below is or ought to be just the season for growth. It is the school where we are to learn truth in practice; but then it is the application and deepening in our souls of that which we have already in the grace of God. "I have not written unto you", says the apostle, "because ye know not the truth, but because ye know it, and that no lie is of the truth" (1 John 2:21). This is the portion of every child of God.

But this very privilege indicates the great essential on man's side in order to be a worshipper. Man as such, unless born of God, is incapable of worshipping God— no more able to do so than a horse is capable of understanding science or philosophy. I deny entirely and in principle that there is any capacity in man, as he is naturally, to worship God. He needs to be a new creature in Christ; he needs to possess a new nature that is of God, in order to be able to understand or to worship God. Not that the simple fact of eternal life, which every soul receives in believing on the Son of God, alone qualifies for worship; but then God does not give it alone. He has provided other means of the greatest possible moment, and He has vouchsafed them not merely to some, but to all His children. In many cases however, lamentable to say, the appearance and the enjoyment of this great grace may be hindered. It may be hardly possible to discern either the divine capacity or the power of worship. But we are entitled always to reckon on the Lord, the unfailing truth of His word, and the fulness of His grace.

If God has given a new life to His children, and reconciled them to Himself by Him who has borne their sins in His own body on the tree, wherefore has this great work been done? No doubt for His own glory and out of His own love; but it is as a part of that glory and an answer to His love that He calls upon His children to praise as well as serve Him now. And we have before us the consideration of this very subject—Christian worship, which demands the gift of the Pentecostal Spirit quite as much as either the assembly or ministry can do—a part of the homage of the children of God, and a return of heart which God claims from all that are His.

The first great requisite then for man, in order to worship as a Christian, is that he be born of God as the object of His grace in Christ, and receive the Holy Ghost to dwell in him. The Lord teaches the principle of it in the answer He gives to the Samaritan woman—"If thou knewest the gift of God, and who it is that saith to thee, Give me to drink, thou wouldest have asked of him, and he would have given thee living water." There we have the kernel, as it were, of worship—"If thou knewest the gift of God". It is not the law, were it of God Himself, though even that she knew not as one that was under it; for the Samaritans were a mongrel people, Gentiles really though partially Jewish in profession and form. But even if the law of God had been known in all its fulness, unimpaired and uncorrupted by man, it certainly would not have fitted for Christian worship. But the word was, "if thou knewest the *gift of God*"—His free-giving; if she knew God as a giver—that He is acting out of His free bounty and love. This is the first truth. But in the next place, "If thou knewest . . . . *who* it is that saith to thee, Give me to drink, thou wouldest have asked of him, and he would have given thee living water."

All the time God sanctioned the law as a system, He dwelt in thick darkness; that is, He did not reveal but hide Himself, as it were. But when the only-begotten Son declared the Father, God no longer occupied the position of a claimant on man, which was necessarily the form in which the law presented His character. Of course this character was right and just and good, like the commandment itself; and man ought to have bowed to Him and answered His demand. But man was a sinner; and the effect of pressing the claim was to bring out more plainly the sins of man. Had the law been the image of God, as ignorant and perverse theologians falsely teach, man must have been hopelessly left and lost. But this was far from the truth. The law, though of God, is neither God nor a reflection of God, but only the moral measure of what sinful man owes to God. God is light; God is love; and if man is in the depth of need, He gives freely, fully, like Himself. Indeed it is what becomes Him, and what He delights in. "It is more blessed to give than to receive." It were strange if God were defrauded of that which is the more blessed of the two. According to the law He should have been a receiver, had not man broken down; in the Gospel He is unequivocally a giver, and what is more, a giver of His very best to those whose only desert is everlasting destruction.

But this is only possible through the glory and the humiliation of the Son of God, stooping down and suffering to the uttermost for sinners. How truly and beautifully then the Lord says, "If thou knewest the gift of God, and who it is that saith to thee, Give me to drink, thou wouldest have asked of him, and he would have given thee living water": in other words, had she known God's grace and the glory of Him who freely talked with her, she would have sought and found all she wanted. Little did she suspect who the lowly One was whom she supposed to be but a Jew, though she did wonder that a Jew could be so tender and so bend down to a Samaritan woman. Little did she think that it was the Lord God of heaven and earth, the only-begotten in the bosom of the Father; had she known but a little of this, she would have asked, and He would have given her living water. It is the Holy Ghost that is meant by the "living water". Thus in a single verse we have the whole Trinity in one way or another concerned. God's own grace is the first thought, the source; then we have the glory of the Person of the Son, and His presence in humiliation among men on the earth; finally the Son according to His proper glory gives to needy thirsty souls the living water—the Holy Ghost. Is it necessary to say that none but a person supremely divine could impart such a blessing?

Here then you have testified by our Lord Jesus the necessary basis of Christian worship: first of all, God revealed as He is in the Gospel as contrasted with the law—God in His grace; secondly, the Son coming down in perfect goodness, and willing to be man's debtor in the least things that He might bless him in the greatest by a love which can win the most careless and obdurate; and thirdly, the gift of the Holy Ghost. What must

Christian worship be according to its true character and
object in the mind of God, if all these things are necessary in order that it should exist! It does in very deed
suppose on God's part a full revelation of what He is in
His own nature and in His grace to man. It does assume
that the Son has come amongst men in love to make
good that revelation in the thorough putting away of sin
by the sacrifice of Himself. It also supposes that the
heart, awakened to its real wants, has asked and received
of the Lord living water, the Holy Ghost, not only as the
agent of life and renewal, but as a well within of unfailing refreshment springing up into everlasting life.

Accordingly a little lower down in the chapter we have
more developed instruction on the subject, although we
have had the foundation of it in verse 10. The woman,
when her conscience was touched, and she learned that
she stood in the presence of a prophet, though not yet
recognizing in Him the Messiah, put her religious difficulties before Him for solution, quite sure that He
brought the truth of God—"I perceive that thou art a
prophet." Remark in passing that the essential idea of a
prophet, both in the Old and the New Testament sense,
is one that brings the conscience directly into the presence of God, so as to have His light shed upon the soul.
There were many prophets who predicted scarcely anything, but they were not the less prophets. Finding
herself then in the presence of one who was able to
announce the truth of God, she wants to have the questions of her soul answered. She turned to Him about
that which at all times and everywhere has and must
have unrivalled interest. The world itself, blind and
dead, will fight for nothing faster than its religion. There
were differences then as there are now. "Our fathers",

she said, "worshipped in this mountain; and ye say that in Jerusalem is the place where men ought to worship." The Lord solemnly tells her: "Woman, believe me, the hour cometh when ye shall neither in this mountain nor yet at Jerusalem worship the Father." He gives a rebuke too: "Ye worship ye know not what. We know what we worship, for salvation is of the Jews." It is clear that whatever hopes of salvation were held out to the Jews, they were founded on their belief in Christ. But while He vindicates the position (not the condition) of the Jews, He proclaims the dawn of a brighter day: "The hour cometh, and now is, when the true worshippers shall worship the Father in spirit and in truth, for the Father seeketh such to worship him." He could speak thus plainly and strongly because He was Himself the Son in the bosom of the Father, and was entitled, in virtue of the glory of His Person, to bring in worship suited to His own intimate knowledge and perfect revelation of the Father.

Thereon at once follows the full and distinctive character of Christian worship. God is made known as a Father calling and adopting children; nay, more than this, He is *seeking* children. In this is the fulness of divine love going out from heaven and for heaven. In Israel men had to seek Jehovah, and this with carefully prescribed rites and rigid ceremonies: thus only could even the chosen people in their worship come and appear before God. Notwithstanding the nicest care, not one could approach into His presence—nay not even the high priest himself; and if it had been possible for him to draw and stay near, it was not to God revealed as a Father. God was no more Father to Aaron, or Phinehas, or Zadok, than He was to the least member of the most obscure tribe in Israel. There was at that time no such manifestation of God. But now the hour was coming, and in principle come, when the Father was seeking worshippers. The Jewish system had been tried and found wanting, and was now doomed. Before God the worldly sanctuary was already fallen, and Christ was the true temple. The Son of God was come, and this could not but change all things—not only teach, but change all. No wonder then that there was, in and through His presence, a new and full display of God, a declaration of the Father's name. Here Christ makes known the new thing in this point of view; how earthly worship must vanish, not merely at the mountain of Gerizim, but even in Jerusalem; that it was a question henceforth of worshipping the Father, and this in spirit and in truth; for, wondrous to say, the Father was *seeking* such to worship Him!

What a truth! God the Father going out in His own uncaused, creative love in quest of worshippers! Of course, He was accomplishing this task by His Son, and in the energy of the Holy Spirit. Still, this was the principle, in direct contrast with nature and Judaism—the Father seeking worshippers. Not only was it an entirely new character of worship, suited to and demanding the new revelation of God Himself, but it necessarily and completely extinguished the old lamps of the sanctuary hitherto acknowledged in Jewry. Not only was the spurious worship of Samaria more than ever condemned, but the brightness of heaven, now shining freely, eclipsed the feeble rays which in Israel were meant at least to make the darkness visible, and to keep up a testimony to better light that was coming. What had been temporarily owned and used of God was now becoming a nullity and a nuisance; and God, as we might expect, brought in the vast change most righteously. Up to this time man was on his trial. The Jew, as the sample of chosen, favoured man, was being proved; and what was the issue of it? The cross and shame of the Lord Jesus. They rejected and slew their own Messiah, little knowing too, that He was Jehovah, God over all, blessed for ever. Justly therefore and after long patience the Jews were put aside. Such was the moral development of the ways of God. There was nothing arbitrary, as every one who believes what God declares in His word as to Israel's rejection of the Messiah must at once see and feel. In the life and ministry of Christ was a manifestation of such grace and long-suffering as had never been witnessed or even conceived on the earth. But now the end was come before God. The Jews, by their conduct, were cutting the last ties which a people in the flesh could have with God. In rejecting their Messiah they rejected themselves. But when the cross was a fact, and redemption accomplished, when Jesus was risen from the dead, the grace and truth which had come by Him shone out in His work on the cross, and the plenteous redemption, not promised now, but accomplished, was made known by the Holy Ghost. Accordingly those who believed were in a capacity to worship the Father. It is not merely that they had faith in the Messiah, for this they had when He was here. But now that they had in Him redemption through His blood, the forgiveness of sins; now that Christ made God Himself known as His Father and their Father, His God and their God (and this in the power and presence of the Holy Ghost sent down from heaven), they could draw near into the holiest, and truly worship the true God; they could say, not only by, but with the Lord Jesus, "Abba, Father."

Not merely were spiritual life and redemption needful, but the Holy Ghost also; and accordingly here the Lord adds that "God is a Spirit: and they that worship him must worship him in spirit and in truth." Mark the difference of the language. When He speaks of His Father seeking worshippers, it is pure grace flowing freely out; it is *He* who is seeking. It is not merely that He accepts the worship of His people, but He seeks worshippers. Yet let us remember that our Father is God. It is a thing easily forgotten, strange to say; but this is mere fleshliness, and not from our privilege in infinite mercy of nearness to Him, which ought not in the least degree to dull, but to increase and strengthen our sense of His majesty. "God is a Spirit", He says; "and they that worship him *must* worship him in spirit and in truth." There is a certain moral necessity here, which cannot be dispensed with. The truth is, Christ creates, the law never does. The law kills; what else can it do or ought it to do for sinful creatures? It would be a bad law if it did let us off. If I deserve to die as a guilty man responsible to God, then, I say, the law is just, holy, and good in condemning me. It is the province of the Saviour alone to give me life, and not this merely, but to give me life by His death and resurrection, without sin, fruit or root, that I may stand in Him possessed of a new nature, wholly delivered by grace from the misery, guilt, power, and judgment of the old man.

This is the place of every Christian. These are the simple but most blessed elements of his life and standing before God; but then, as they are inseparable from the gift of the Holy Ghost, so is He absolutely needed that we may worship our God and Father; and for this purpose and others He is given. Thus we see what the living water means. "The water that I shall give him shall be in him a well of water springing up into everlasting life." It is the Holy Ghost given by Christ to be *in* the believer;

without Him there can be no such thing as the power of worship. But He is given, and the hour of true Christian worship is come in the strictest sense.

And you that are here assembled to-night, are you prepared to acknowledge, for any consideration whatever, worship which is not of this character? You, especially, who are young in years, and perhaps, also, little established in the truth of God, hearken. You may be tempted, not only through natural hankering after the world and its worship, but you have relatives, connexions, friends, who think it hard you do not join them. In what? In Christian worship? Join them in it by all means. Whenever, wherever you find worship in spirit and in truth, fear not to join; seek it, yes, earnestly seek it. Rather would I ask, are you disposed to slight such worship for that which does all it can to return to the mountain of Samaria, if it cannot reach Jerusalem; for a religious service that is both untrue and formal; and an order that mingles some genuine worshippers in a crowd of false? How many there are now-a-days who, in word boasting of their heavenly liturgy, in reality hurry through it with such evident heedlessness as to show that the sermon is all they care to hear! One might fancy they were men who knew nothing, desired nothing, but to hear the way to be saved, instead of being God's children, called and capacitated to worship the Father in spirit and in truth. But this is the misery of being in a position which is bound up with what they value in the flesh and in the world; where worshipping the Father according to His word never was nor can be known.

I admit that even this is better than belonging to another class of religionists, nominally in the same sect, who, being ignorant of Christ's redemption, bear with an evangelical discourse for the sake of services, the darkness of which is to them delightful, because it answers to their own condition. Fleshly worship suits a fleshly state.

My charge is not about the slipping in of a hypocrite amongst the true—these no doubt may creep in anywhere. The main point insisted on is the error and sin of embracing the world in divine worship through a false principle, than which there is nothing in the present day more common, and in some eyes more desirable. Clearly this is not Christian worship; but still it is so styled; it is accepted and justified as such; and the refusal of it is branded popularly as the fruit of a harsh unloving censorious spirit, instead of being seen to be, as it is, simple-hearted desire to carry out the will of the Lord. Worship there cannot be, unless the ground of grace is taken: there must be life in the Spirit, nothing less than divine life and the power of the Holy Ghost working in the worshipper.

Again, it ought not to be very difficult to discern where there is Christian worship. One can easily say where it is not. How can it be where there is no recognition of the assembly of the faithful in separation from the world? where human formularies largely displace the divine word? where the Holy Ghost is not welcomed to work in the order laid down in scripture? where anybody may be in membership, and the evidently unconverted can join in or lead the most serious services? The invariable effect is that as you cannot raise the world to the height of faith, the believers who mingle all together indiscriminately must descend to the world's level. Hence, fine buildings, imposing ceremonies, exciting music, poetic sentiment, are apt to come in by degrees, where Christian worship is unknown or forgotten. Hence too the need of legal order, for it seems bold to trust the grace of God.

You may have Christian worshippers in such a state of things; for I have no desire to exaggerate; but Christian worship there cannot be. Do you doubt this? Perhaps the doubt is because you have never known what worship really is. So much is this the case at present—the thoughts of Christians are so vague, unformed, and dark—that to many the very meaning of worship is lost. How many call a building where they meet to hear preaching a place of worship; and when they go to hear, they think and say they are going to worship! Does not all this show that the very idea of worship is unknown? Nor is it to be wondered at. The truth is, there is a great deal of preaching of Christ in these days, much calculated to arouse and also to win souls; but where is there a full setting forth of the Gospel of God's grace? That Christ is preached at all is a matter for which we have to thank God. Souls are converted, and learn, as far as the usual orthodox testimony goes, what is most true of their sins and their danger; but we want the gospel of God fully proclaimed—the gospel as we see it set forth in the epistles—the glad news not only that the work of Christ has put sin away, but that the believer stands in a new life and relationship with God, of which the Holy Ghost is given as the seal. Where this is known, worship is the simple necessary fruit; the heart, thus set free by grace, goes out to God in thanksgiving and praise.

So in the chapter we began with, the believer enjoys not only a new life communicated, but a well of water within him, which springs up into everlasting life. Thus, by the energy of the Holy Spirit given to us, we possess, as a conscious thing, perfect, unbroken peace, and we cannot but breathe the joy of our ransomed souls to the praise of our Saviour God. As a fact this may not be found among the children of God, save few comparatively; because in general, where there is a perception of Christ, they put the law in the place of the Holy Ghost, and thus fall into the uncertainty which invariably, where there is conscience, flows from the law thus misused, instead of enjoying the light, and power, and peace in Christ and His redemption, which is the proper fruit of the Holy Ghost's testimony to Christ and of His indwelling in the believer. Here only can you have Christian worship. It is founded upon the full revelation of grace in Christ dead, risen, and ascended; and it is in the power of the Spirit of God that this is enjoyed by the believer. But not this only: for God is a Spirit, and the consequence is, that Christian worship repudiates formality. "God is a Spirit: and they that worship him must worship him *in spirit and in truth.*" There we have the nature of God revealed, and thence is deduced the moral need of worshipping Him in spirit and truth, not according to earthly form or human will.

This then is the source, groundwork, and character of Christian worship. But we have one element more when we pursue the further instructions of the New Testament. In 1 Corinthians 14 we find it connected with the assembly. We learn there on what principle, and by whom, worship is now paid to God. This is an important addition to our knowledge of God's will. No one contends for a moment that the gospel should not be preached, or that believers should not be instructed in the truth. These are duties confessedly according to scripture. There we have everything provided for, that can be needed for the good of the Church, and for the well-being of souls; we have both the principle and the fact of all Christian service most clearly laid down in the word of God. Among the rest there is no lack of testimony to the manner according to which Christian worship should be conducted. We have seen that none can render acceptable worship to God but Christians: from it the world is plainly shut out, according to the teaching of scripture. It is not a question of closing the door, or of excluding persons from the place where the faithful assemble. It is clear from scripture that unbelievers might be present where the assembly of God may be gathered; but they are incapacitated from rendering proper and acceptable worship unto God, because they have neither the new nature, nor the Holy Spirit, who is the only power of worship; they neither know redemption, which is the basis of worship, nor do they know the God and Father of our Lord Jesus, who, with the Son, is the object of worship. Thus, in every point of view, the world is necessarily without the pale of Christian worship, and the bringing the world in is a large part of the sin and ruin of Christendom.

Again we gather from 1 Corinthians 14 the place which the giving of thanks has in the worship of God; and this connected, not with any one individual only, or a separate class, but with the order and operation of God in the assembly. Hence we read (verse 15), "What is it then? I will pray with the spirit, and I will pray with the understanding also: I will sing with the spirit, and I will sing with the understanding also." Important as singing is, its end is not, of course, the sweet sound: the essential thing, as we are told, is "singing with the spirit and understanding also". What a proof that the Lord is looking for the intelligent service of His people! So in verse 16 we read, "Else when thou shalt bless with the spirit, how shall he that occupieth the room of the unlearned say Amen at thy giving of thanks, seeing he understandeth not what thou sayest?" If in Christian worship there were the utterance of an unknown tongue in the giving of thanks or in blessing God, it would traverse the rules of edifying the assembly, because it would leave out those that could not intelligently join their "Amen". The passage is cited also to show that thanksgiving and blessing, like singing, and other constituents of Christian worship known to us familiarly, were found from the first in the Christian assembly.

But there is just the difficulty. Look right or left—look where you will, where can you find the Christian assembly? Where is there the gathering together of the children of God in the name of the Lord Jesus engaged in thanksgiving and blessing, praising and singing, as we read of here? Yet the assembly of God, meeting as such, is essential to Christian worship. There might be the best of men chosen to conduct the service, and the order of praise and prayer might be as faultless as existing liturgies are open to severe criticism; but what then? Would it be the worship of the family of God? If not, how could it be of really Christian character? God looks for the worship of His children in the Spirit. Do you say that after all it is only the slight difference of several taking part, instead of one? But grave as that might be, such a difference is not the essential thing, but this—that there be perfect openness for the Spirit's action by whom He is pleased to speak. It is not then a question of one man, or half-a-dozen. On some occasions the Holy Ghost might use one or two; on others, more than six in various ways. What scripture demands is, that there be faith in the Spirit's presence, proved by leaving Him His due right to employ as may please Him. It is not therefore a mere question of one, or few, or many mouthpieces to give thanks, or bless, or take part in acts of Christian worship. The real and essential feature is, that the Holy Ghost, being present, should be counted on, and His employment of this Christian or that as He will. In an assembly where there were many spiritual men, it would have a strange appearance if but one or two took an active part in the worship of the Lord. Still, whether few or many speak at any given time, the only scriptural mode by which acceptable worship is rendered is where the whole assembly unites in the liberty of the Spirit, with heart and mind, in the offering of their praises and thanksgivings to God through the Lord Jesus Christ. The Holy Ghost, acting in the assembly by its members may think fit to employ one or twelve to speak the praises suitable to His mind, and according to the condition of the assembly. And what can be sweeter to all, whether or not they be thus employed as the audible channels of worship, than to have the consciousness that the Holy Ghost in very deed so deigns to guide in one and all? The one point of value is, that *He* should be free to direct all for the glory of Christ.

There is another remark of a practical kind to be made as to worship. We must guard against bringing into the assembly our own thoughts of the worship to be offered unto God. An individual may give out a hymn to be sung in which he delights, and which may be not only beautiful but true and spiritual in itself; but it may be a mistake in him to give it out—a wholly unsuitable hymn for the occasion on which he desires it to be sung. Again, there may be some outside the assembly, known or unknown, who, out of curiosity, are come to see what the worship is like. Now are you, fearing that they might wonder at the silence from time to time, to read a chapter, or give out some sweet hymn? Need I say that such a step is indefensible, and beneath men who believe in the presence of the Holy Ghost? Some may think there is liberty to do this or the like; but who put such thoughts into the mind? Do you think the Holy Spirit is occupied with what those without may say or think of those within, or anything of the kind? Is He not on the contrary filled with His own thoughts of Christ, and communicating them to us? The becoming thing, therefore, for us to do under such circumstances is to look from ourselves, and those within and without, to God, that He, working by the Spirit, may give us communion with the present thoughts of the Spirit of God about the Lord Jesus Christ.

When such is the case, how simple is the flow of thanksgiving for His special mercies to us and all saints! how fragrant the sense God gives us of His delight in Christ! what praise of His grace! what anticipations of glory, and of Christ Himself there! All these and more are but ingredients; and they will variously predominate as the Lord sees fit. Even a lower character of worship, if it be but suited to a given state, is, in my judgment, a far more pleasing thing to God than any strain ever so high, which has not the real present energy of the Spirit of God connected with it.

Further, as to criticism: I cannot think the assembly of God is the right place for any man to stand up and show his superior wisdom in; on the contrary, therein, above all occasions, is the place for the greatest to show his littleness before God. There may be seasons and circumstances where a judgment of what is given out may not be amiss, but a duty; but the assembly of God is not the place for such a course. May I not take the liberty of applying to this what the apostle lays down as to another innovation: "If any man seem to be contentious, we have no such custom, neither the assemblies of God"? How, where, could any one gather such a practice from the word of God? Nor do I confine myself here, or in these remarks generally, to a bare text, but I am speaking of the whole tenor, and texture, and object of all that is given us in the scripture. Accordingly, as it is unauthorised, so the result cannot but be pernicious. What can the effect of criticism in the assembly of God be but the sowing of discord and distraction where unity and concord should prevail? And yet it may be a thing too often done; against it I would warn my hearers earnestly. All are liable to make mistakes, and all deserve to be corrected occasionally; but, as a general rule, comment upon another is altogether out of place in the Christian assembly. There is a meet time and place for every real duty; and it never can be right to rectify one wrong by another, however godly the intention.

Next, as to the breaking of bread, a few scriptures will suffice. The Lord's Supper, not baptism, was revealed of the Lord, we all know, to the apostle Paul, as it is brought out in the same epistle (1 Corinthians 11) from which much has been already quoted. It is a holy institution, intimately linked with, and the distinct outward expression of the unity of Christ's body, which it was St. Paul's work especially to develop. We have the Lord accordingly there revealing it afresh to the apostle Paul. He had not sent Paul to baptize, as he says, but to preach the gospel. There is not the least doubt that he did baptize, nor that it was perfectly right in him to baptize. But baptism, so expressly charged on the eleven, after the Lord's resurrection, is not only a single initiatory observance—"one baptism",—but it is for each individual the confession of the foundation-truth of Christ's death and resurrection. The subject of it stands forth as a believer in Him who died and rose; he is no longer therefore a Jew, or a heathen, but a confessor of Christ. The Lord's Supper, on the other hand, belongs to the assembly, and forms an affecting and important object in the worship of the saints of God. It is primarily and strictly the standing sign of our only foundation; it is the witness of His love unto death, and His work, by virtue of which such as we can worship. No wonder therefore we have the apostle Paul showing the very solemn and blessed place which the Lord's Supper claims in the revelations of the Lord to him. "I have received of the Lord that which also I delivered unto you, that the Lord Jesus, the same night in which he was betrayed, took bread: and when he had given thanks, he brake it, and said, Take, eat: this is my body, which is broken for you: this do in remembrance of me. After the same manner also he took the cup, when he had supped, saying, This cup is the new testament in my blood: this do ye, as oft as ye drink it, in remembrance of me. For as often as ye eat this bread, and drink this cup, ye do show the Lord's death till he come." It is evident, on the face of the state-ment, what a large and deep place the Lord's death has in His Supper. No joy, no brightness of the favour of God in heaven, no consequent communion, nor hopes of everlasting blessedness with Him, can be allowed for a moment to distract from, or overshadow, the death of the Lord. But the reverse is the truth; for the more the Lord's death has its own central value before the Christian, all these things shine out not only more brightly but also more sweetly and affectingly to the heart. And so the same man who was God's blessed instrument for developing the full extent of the Christian's privileges, is the very one who gathers us around our Lord's death as that which pre-eminently attracts and fills every heart that loves His name.

From Acts 20:7, it is plain that the saints should break bread on the first day of the week, not of the month or quarter. But it is the resurrection day, not the day of His death, as if we were summoned to be there in mourning as for the dead. But He is risen, and therefore, with grateful, solemn joy, we take the Supper on the day that speaks of His rising power. I cannot but believe that the Holy Ghost records the day for our instruction, as well as the object that called together the believers primarily. No doubt the apostle, passing through after a short stay, discoursed to those assembled; but they came together on that day to break bread. Have we consented to other thoughts and arrangements? Or do we act as if we believed the Holy Spirit knows and shows us the best and truest, the holiest and happiest way of pleasing God and honouring Christ? The death of the Lord keeps constantly before the soul our utter need as once guilty sinners, proved by the cross; the complete blotting out of all our sins by His blood; the glorifying of God up to, and above all in, death itself; the manifestation of absolute grace, and withal the righteousness of God in justifying us; the perfect glory of the Saviour;—all these things, and infinitely more, are brought and kept before us in those simple but wondrous words—"the Lord's death"!

To take the Supper in remembrance of the Lord, and thus show forth His death, is what gathers us together as our prime desire. There can be no doubt about the meaning of the word of God which records this for our comfort and edifying; yet how could one infer that such was His will if one looked at the practice of Christians? Compare what they are doing Lord's-day after Lord's-day, with the obvious lessons of scripture, and intention of the Lord in so revealing His mind to us; and say whether for the most part this simple, touching memorial has not been slighted by real saints, and whether its character has not been changed universally in Christendom. I speak not of points of form, but of its principle—of such an interference with its mode of celebration as leaves hardly a single shred according to the Lord's institution.

Beware of thinking anything can be of equal moment with duly showing forth the Lord's death. The Supper of the Lord claims an unequivocal prominence in the worship of the saints. Not that one thinks of the mere fact of celebrating it, as to time, in the middle of the meeting. Indeed, it is remarkable how the Spirit of God avoids laying down laws about the Supper (and the same is true of Christianity in general)—a circumstance which the unfaithful may abuse, but which gives infinitely greater scope to the spirit of Christian affection and obedience. This however we may safely say, that it is not a question of the point of time when the act of breaking the bread occurs. The all-important thing is, that the Lord's Supper should be the governing thought when the saints are gathered for this purpose on the Lord's day; that neither the prayers of many, nor the teaching of any, should put that great object in the shade. In ministry however spiritual, man has his place; in the Supper, if rightly celebrated, the abased Lord alone is exalted. There might be occasions where the evident guidance of the Spirit brings it early before us, or postpones it late in the meeting, and thus any technical rule binding it to the beginning, or middle, or end, would be human encroachment on Him who alone is competent on each occasion and always to decide.

This openness may seem strange to such as are habituated to rigid forms, even where there are no written formularies; but that apparent strangeness is chiefly due to their habitual lack of acquaintance with the real presence and guidance of the Holy Ghost in the assembly. Where however the door is open to the action of the Spirit according to scripture, and where a just sense of what is in hand pervades the assembly, the Spirit of God, somehow or another, according to the truth of things in His sight, knows how to adjust the right moment as well as all else, and to give us the comfort of His guidance, if the Lord be but the confidence of our souls.

Again it may be that you sometimes go to the Lord's table and return disappointed, because there has been no exposition of the word, or no exhortation. Is it possible that you have gone to remember and show forth the death of Christ, and yet have come back with feelings of dissatisfaction? How can this be? Is it not the morbid influence of the present state of Christendom? No doubt there is that in the natural heart which suits and likes what is now the vogue; and the excitement of Egypt's food is readily craved, where the heavenly manna is loathed as light food. Unquestionably we have that within which helps what is found outside; still it is humbling and afflicting to my own mind that a discourse should seem indispensable to garnish the breaking of bread, and that there should be a thought of want in the meeting where the Lord's death has been before the heart; when one has met around the Lord in His own name with those that love Him! Do you suppose that there is any service more acceptable to God Himself than the simple remembrance of Christ in His own Supper?

But, however that may be estimated, all this has been often and plainly forgotten, and the Supper of the Lord has not only been made, in many instances, a much rarer thing than scripture warrants, but its proper character has been tampered with, and the great landmarks that the Lord laid down have been utterly disregarded, so that the celebration is become anything men please to call it, except the Lord's Supper. Say that it is a sacrament, if you will; but one may perhaps doubt that, if so, it is the Lord's Supper. The Corinthians used to take a common meal together on the Lord's day; for in those days Christians strongly felt the social character of Christianity, and one may regret that it has been ever since so much lost sight of. After the meal they celebrated the Lord's Supper. The devil, however, contrived to bring shame and confusion among them at Corinth by license at this feast; some of them got intoxicated. No doubt it was a dreadful dishonour on the Lord's name; but it ill becomes those to speak harshly who are apt to utter the loudest reproaches. We must remember that in those days they had just been brought out of heathenism; and it used to be a part of the worship of false gods to get drunk in their honour. The Gentiles did not feel the immorality of it in the way that everybody knows now. It was thought no improper thing then to be thus excited and worse in their religious rites, and, indeed, at other times. It is probable therefore, that in this infant assembly at Corinth it was not counted such an enormity as we know it to be, that Christians should so far forget the Lord at the *agape*. What aggravated the sin was the mixing up the Lord's Supper then and there, it seems, with the love-feast. Such conduct was destructive of the character of His Supper. To eat and drink thus was to eat judgment (1 Corinthians 11:29). What had been begun in the Spirit ended in the flesh. I refer to this merely for the purpose of showing that, by bringing carnal feasting into such a holy assemblage, we lose or destroy its true nature and aim.

Thus, without confining oneself to the notice of any particular body, the practice of appointing particular officials, whose sole right and title[5] it is to administer the bread and wine to each communicant, is clean contrary to the teaching of Scripture, and flies in the face of the evident intention of God, quite as much as the distressing conduct of the Corinthians themselves. For what is the Lord's Supper? Is it not the family feast? When you derange the Father's order among the members of His family, or when you bring in those that are not of His family, its character is gone, it is the family feast no more. Let us then assume the least unfavourable supposition of a Christian company, and of none but Christians. Yet supposing that the administration, as men call it, of the Supper of the Lord is committed to a real minister of Christ, or to all who are His ministers, as the exclusive prerogative of such as minister only—I put the most favourable form which can be conceived for the popular notion—under any and all circumstances, it is a human invention, not only without the authority of Christ, but decidedly contrary to the doctrine and facts recorded in scripture. I admit ministry most fully; but the Lord's Supper has no connexion with it. Make it a necessary function of those that rule to administer the bread and wine, and it bears not even an outward resemblance to the Lord's Supper. It becomes a sacrament, not His Supper; a manifest innovation, a decided and complete departure from what the Lord has laid down in His word. The very idea of a person standing apart and claiming to administer it as a right alters and ruins the Supper of the Lord. That Supper, according to scripture, leaves no room for the display of human importance in the pretensions of a clergy; least of all when the apostles were on earth. Blessed and honoured of God as these were at the celebration of the Lord's Supper, they were there in His presence as souls that were saved from sin and its judgment by the Lord's death. In the regulation of the churches, in the choice of elders, in the appointment of deacons, they had their own proper place of apostolic dignity. The word of God clearly and fully proves that the administration of the Supper by an official is a figment and tradition of men, wholly wanting the support of scripture.

But there is another point that often troubles souls, and might possibly harass, even where the bread is broken in a holy simple scriptural manner—the danger of eating unworthily, and so of incurring "damnation". Let me meet this at once by the assurance that, though one has to watch against a careless or otherwise unworthy participation, there is no thought of damnation, which would indeed upset for the believer all the comfort of the gospel and the general drift of God's word. But some may say, "Do not the scriptures assert as much?" I admit the English version does, but not the word of God; and we must not confound them. We have every reason to thank God for the English Bible, which, as far as I am acquainted with the subject, I believe to be as good a version, if not better than any other current in the world; but for all this, it is only a version, and therefore a work in which the weakness of man appears, and in which are found here and there defects which human infirmity has not been able to avoid. One of these errors is on this very subject (in 1 Corinthians 11:29). The apostle is showing how essential it is that we go to the Lord's table, which invites us freely as every week opens, our hearts filled with grateful remembrance of Christ's self-sacrificing love, who died in atonement that we through Him might be saved. What is the result of a light heedless state at the Lord's Supper? If we take the bread and wine at that holy feast as we eat the common food God provides in our own houses, not discerning the Lord's body—in other words, if we eat and drink unworthily, it is not the Lord's Supper we are eating, but rather judgment to ourselves. The Lord's hand will be on such, as the apostle shows by the case of the disorderly Corinthians; but even in that aggravated instance, it was expressly temporal judgment, that they should *not* be damned or "condemned with the world". On the other hand, there is no excuse for absenting yourself from the Lord's table. There is no escape from the hand of the Lord, save by humbling ourselves and vindicating Him by self-judgment, and then coming. The Lord's Supper is no more a sweet privilege than a solemn duty for all His own, save those under discipline; and when we think of the love He has shown us in the boundless sacrifice He has made for us—the deliverance wholly undeserved He has wrought for us in His own deep abasement and suffering under God's wrath on the cross, together with all the gracious encouragement He has therein brought before us for our comfort, admonition, and support in our conflict through the world, we cannot but regard the thankful commemoration of the Lord's death as a paramount obligation which under no circumstances ought to be neglected.

Another person's fault should not keep me away: if it rightly acts so on one, it ought to hinder all. Is the Lord then to be as it were forgotten because somebody deserves censure? Let the faulty individual be reproved or otherwise dealt with according to scripture; but my place is to "*do this* in remembrance of Christ". Again, a sense of my own faultiness should not keep me back. "Let a man examine himself, and *so let him eat*"—not stay away. He who abstains from the Lord's Supper virtually says he is none of His.

This will suffice as to the breaking of bread, barely as the subject has been touched. A few words remain to be added in regard to prayer. There is very often a great mistake made as to this. We hear, sometimes about the "gift of prayer"; but where do you find it? Show me a passage of scripture which speaks of a "gift of prayer" in the sense in which people commonly use the term? What is the effect? It largely hinders conscientious modest simple souls, who otherwise would join heartily in public prayer. But they cannot give themselves credit for possessing the "gift of prayer". They are frightened by what is a mere bugbear—by what is really, if they but knew it, a blunder. The consequence of this for them is, that they hang back, and are silent, when the meeting would be greatly benefited by their help. Are there not some now present who know well that they have had many a time a desire to pray, and thus express the wants of God's assembly to Himself, but who have been deterred because they feared their lack of a "gift of prayer", and that they might not be able to pray long enough, or in a way acceptable to some whom they have heard insisting on the "gift of prayer"? Is it not a fact? I entreat you, beloved friends, to listen to them no more, nor heed your own thoughts and feelings.

Examine the word of God for yourselves, and you will find that the apostle lays down (1 Timothy 2), and even peremptorily, his desire that the men pray everywhere.

Let them then commit themselves to the Lord without doubt, and at the same time remember, that scripture at any rate never even hints about a "gift of prayer". This brings us to another point connected with the one I have just endeavoured to explain. It is in my opinion a mischievous notion, that those who possess a ministerial gift should be regarded as the only proper persons to let their voices be heard in the assembly of God.

Lecture 5:
Gifts and Local Charges

EPHESIANS 4:7-11

I should feel to-night that my subject was dry indeed and promised little profit to souls, if we had only to look at gifts and offices in themselves. It is thus that the subject is often regarded, and is therefore apt to become not only a barren speculative question for some souls, but also a snare to others—barren to such as, looking upon it from outside, think that they at least have nothing to do with gifts and offices, and a snare perhaps as often to those who conclude that they themselves are especially, if not exclusively, concerned in them. The truth is, these spiritual functions closely and materially affect both Christ and the church of God. Attached to Christ as their source, they (at any rate gifts) flow down from the same reservoir of rich grace on high, whence all the main characteristic blessings of the church proceed. They proceed from Him in heavenly places, and therein is the true answer to much, the greater part, of the aversion some feel to the subject, as if ministerial gifts were only a means of giving importance to their possessors. It would be hard to think that such a turn can be anything but a gross perversion of what comes from Christ or heaven. In truth they are of the deepest moment in God's eyes, as He deigns to use them for the glory of His Son; and surely the consideration of the light that scripture affords should be precious to those whose joy as well as responsibility it is to profit by them; and not least to those who have personally and most jealously to watch how the gift of Christ's grace is used, lest it should be diverted from the object for which the Lord gave it to some selfish or worldly account. It is evident, I think, that simply to state the source is, in the principle of it, to cut off all excuse for the earthly aggrandisement, in various forms, which the Lord's gifts are too commonly made to serve.

But then there is another remark to be made. Not only do these gifts of Christ spring from Him in heaven, and therefore must, if anything can, refuse to mingle with the vanity of the world and the pride of man (I speak, of course, of the gift itself, and not of the flesh's perversion of it); but besides there is another feature of these gifts, which is of immense interest to us as believers in the Lord Jesus. They are essentially bound up with Christianity, not on the contemplative side, but in what is equally needful, its active and aggressive character. But whether you look at the source or the character, all is founded on an eternal redemption that is already accomplished. The more these considerations are weighed, the more their importance will appear; the more also, it seems to me, the subject of the gifts of Christ will be seen to be entirely above that earthly and barren domain to which theology at least would consign it.

Further, is there not a wrong done to God and His saints, wherever that which the Lord deigned to make known to us in His word—that which constitutes, rightly applied, so essential a part of the blessing of the church—is viewed as but a secondary matter that can be taken up or laid aside at will? In point of fact, such indifference to His truth is deep dishonour done to Him, and a corresponding loss invariably to the souls of the saints who thus slight His will. It must be evident, if it were only from the scripture just read, that the Holy Ghost does not in any way banish the subject of gifts into some dark corner—if such there can be in the scriptures— whence we may, if we please, draw it forth from time to time, and wield it to the best account of our party. In the Epistle to the Ephesians, where the Holy Ghost has shown both heights and depths of blessing in Christ and in the church—in the very centre where He shows us too the Lord Himself in His own glory at the right hand of God—it is there beyond almost any other part of the New Testament, that we find the Spirit launching out into an account of the gifts of the Lord to the church.

But, observe, I say the "gifts *of the Lord*", because so it is that they are regarded here, rather than gifts *of the Spirit*. Indeed it would be difficult to find such an expression in scripture. There is a passage which seems to say as much in Hebrews 2; but it is properly "the distributions of the Holy Ghost". You will find also in 1 Corinthians 12 that wisdom, knowledge, and the rest are said to be given by "the same Spirit". But still, in these things, the Holy Ghost, properly speaking, is not regarded as the giver, save mediately. The Lord is the real and proper giver; the Spirit of God is rather the intermediate means of conveying the gift, distributing or making it good,— the energy by which the Lord acts. And I conceive it to be of moment, practically, that we should see that the gifts which are used to call out and build up the church, and which are the only true basis of ministry, take their rise from Christ Himself.

Ministry then may be defined to be the exercise of gift, and therefore it is evident that these gifts of grace are bound up with it in the most intimate manner. There can be no ministry of the word (properly speaking) without gift by the Spirit from Christ.

But let us look for a moment at the development which the Holy Ghost gives to the truth that these gifts flow from Christ. "Unto every one of us is given grace according to the measure of the gift of Christ." It is not a bare question of qualities possessed; still less is it merely a matter of attainment, let it be ever so well meant to give honour to the Holy Ghost. It is a new thing given, the positive consequence of grace; it is the fruit of the free favour of the Lord, who in these things acts according to His own sovereign will and for the glory of God.

"And unto every one [or each] of us is given grace according to the measure of the gift of Christ. Wherefore he saith, [taking up Psalm 68] 'When he ascended up on high, he led captivity captive, and gave gifts unto men.'" Although the Lord Jesus was in His person, one need hardly say, competent at all times, still He was pleased, in the order of the ways of God, to wait for the great work to be done—and done too, not merely as regarded man in divine mercy towards him, but in view of the enemy who was to be dealt with; the power must be broken that had led captive the children of God. Hence the spiritual enemies were first disposed of, and the Lord is accordingly represented here as ascending up to heaven on the defeat, the total defeat before God, of all the once mighty unseen power of evil. Upon this foundation ministry is built. The Lord Jesus goes up into heaven. He has Himself confronted and defeated the powers of darkness. He has led captivity captive; and thereon "He gave gifts to men." How completely the door for man's energy and ambition is closed! How carefully God—alone able to teach us on this subject, and in His revealed word having, in fact, given us the perfect truth—shows us the Lord Jesus, from first to last, the one means of good to us, and glory to God the Father by the Holy Ghost! Do you view Him only as Saviour and Lord? The truth is, there is not a single seed of the Church's blessing, there is not a means of acting upon the souls of ourselves or of others, that is not, every whit of it, connected with Christ. Where we have not apprehended this vital all-embracing connexion with Him, and where that which assumes to be ministry, for instance, does not flow from Him only, it is clear there is a something not to be held fast, but on the contrary to be got rid of; an object not to be fought for as if it were a prize, but to be suspected as contraband, brought into the light of God, and judged in His presence. For whose ministry is it if it be not of the Lord Christ? and for what are we contending if it be not for the gifts of Christ?

The Lord then is ascended on high, and from that height of bliss and glory He has given gifts to men, and the Spirit of God carefully turns aside for a little, and puts us in the very presence of the mighty work on the ground of which Christ took His seat there. "Now that he ascended, what is it but that He also descended first into the lower parts of the earth?" What grace in Him! What infinite love to us, that He might bless us—eternally bless us! He had, with the Father and the Spirit, a divine co-equal right to that place of supreme majesty. They alone were competent to fill it. But He descended first into the lower parts of the earth. He had the highest place above, if I may say so, naturally and intrinsically. It belonged to Him as the Son of God, who counted it not robbery to be equal with God; but He deigned to be made flesh; for, as a part of the counsels of God, it was needful that He should be man. Without the incarnation there could have been no retrieving of the universal ruin of man, and of the dishonour of God through sin; there could have been neither defeat of Satan, nor an adequate and righteous deliverance for man. But now He descends first into the lower parts of the earth. He takes upon Him the sorrow, the shame, the sin. To have condescended to become man, and to live as He lived rejected and abased on earth, would have been much; but what is this to the cross? He went down to the very uttermost, and in consequence of this humiliation, He is now as man exalted to the highest. In His death He retrieved all that was ruined—indeed, I may say, infinitely more. He "restored that which he took not away". He brought a new and better glory to God than had ever been thought or even prophesied of in any respect; for I fear not to say that, as all types and shadows are but the feeble heralds of His glory, so too there is, there could be, no prediction rising up to the height of blessing that was found in Christ, nor fathoming the depth of His moral glory in the sight of God. Himself was needed to come forth—Himself needed that the full worth of His sufferings and cross might be known. Before that there could be no sufficient expression of His glory. It was out of this descent into the lower parts of the earth that He went up—out of this thorough coming down by Him who was as truly God as man, in the very nature which before had borne such fruits of shame and disgrace to God.

But what a change! Humanity is a nature in which the blessed God could delight, as He looked upon it in the Lord Jesus. Now too He ascends; and this, not as He came down; for, descending simply as the Son of God to become the Son of man, He goes up, not the Son of God only, but also the Son of man. Indeed, it is especially in this very character of man that we find Him seated in heaven now. "He ascended up", as it is said, "far above all heavens, that He might fill all things." On this magnificent ground, whether one looks at the humiliation on the one hand, or at the exaltation on the other—on this twofold ground of a height of glory, consequent on a depth of abasement beyond all thought, is founded that ministry which is according to God, being the simple exercise of the gift of Christ. And yet could it be credited, if one did not know it, that there are men, and Christians too, who can look upon such a scene unmoved, if not moved only to spite and sneer and reproach? But it must be so. To work thus belongs to Him whom the world knew not. No wonder therefore that it recognizes not the gifts of His grace. Whatever can be made to merge into the world's greatness, whatever can be altered to suit the age's taste, the world can admire. Even Christianity and the name of Christ—perverted, no doubt, and regarded only in some partial way—may be adopted. Why even the heathen were willing to do it! There was an emperor, as probably many of you know, who would have been glad to put the Lord Jesus as a god in the Pantheon. And so it is now. Has not Christendom something akin for its success? It has taken up piecemeal this institution and that; it has made them the means of adorning the scene into which God "drove out the man", exiled by Him because of sin.

But we who believe are assuredly entitled to look above this world, and there to see, higher than all heavens, our Lord and Master. And what is He doing there? What is His present occupation, according to that which the Spirit of God tells us here? He is giving gifts unto men. Let us bless Him for it! He (Himself a man, for so it is that He has taken this place) is giving gifts unto men. From on high He looks round about upon this world, and His grace makes man to be the vessel of these precious gifts, which savour not only of the person who is there, and of the work He has done, but also of the glory from which He gives them. They are heavenly gifts. They will not, if He be consulted, conform to the world's thought or measure; nor were they ever intended to serve the world but the Lord Jesus, though surely for His sake serving any and every body.

Let us take care then that we truly are subject to Him in whom we believe. And let us beware of the evil heart of unbelief, lest we treat a word of His lightly. Let us remember how easy it is pretending to honour His word, to let it slip away from us, counting it something of the past—no doubt to look back on it with reverential awe, but still as a thing gone by. Is this the living word of a God that lives for ever and ever? Are you going to treat the Head of the church as if He were dead? Nay, He never was dead as the church's Head. Indeed! He only took that Headship as One alive again from the grave, and so giving life; He only took it when both raised from the dead, and gone up to heaven: and yet men act as if the Head of the church were a dead and not a living Lord! And if He is thus living, what is it for? Is it merely as High Priest, according to the Epistle to the Hebrews, to bring His people through the wilderness? There is some tendency in Christians to overlook the priesthood of Christ; but there is a far greater danger of their forgetting Christ as the living Head, who still stands at the fountain-head of blessing, ever in faithful love giving His gifts to man. No doubt it is all summed up as if it were a given thing here—"He *gave*"; and there is a very interesting reason for such a way of presenting His gifts. Assuredly the Lord would not Himself put the gifts of His grace in such a form as to interfere with the church's constant hope of His own return. On the contrary, He would fix the church in the attitude of expecting Himself from heaven. Accordingly not even the supply of ministerial gift is so put as to defer the fulfilment of the "blessed hope" from age to age. On high is the Head of the church, and as Head it is part of His work to vouchsafe all needed gifts for men.

Here then is the whole scene of His grace summed up in one—the Lord gave gifts to men; "and He gave some apostles, and some prophets, and some evangelists, and some pastors and teachers". We have not a catalogue of all the gifts. It is not at all in the manner of scripture or of the Lord to furnish a mere formal list; for the truth is not written in the word of God so as to satisfy human curiosity or form a system of divinity. What is done is infinitely better. He has given us exactly what suited His wisdom in each particular part of scripture. Hence if we compare, for instance, what we have here with the first Epistle to the Corinthians, we shall find striking differences. There are some gifts found here, not there; and some found there which are not here. Now this is not a thing of chance, nor a matter in which the apostle used merely his own judgment and decided things after his own mind. Nobody denies that his heart and mind were deeply exercised. God forbid! But we may bless God that there was an infinitely wise mind directing all things, and that there was a judgment which knew the end from the beginning. We shall find, accordingly, that the apostle mentions these gifts according to that divine intelligence. Indeed, the reason of it, to some extent, may appear as we proceed.

First of all, the gifts (δόματα) here enumerated are in view of the perfecting of the saints, which is the great primary object, branching out into the work of the ministry, and the edifying the body of Christ, as connected with it. Now, there, at once, may be discerned the key, or divine reason for presenting here certain gifts and not others. Here we have nothing, for instance, about speaking in a tongue; neither have we any mention of miracles. Why so? What have they to do with the perfecting the saints? The reason seems to me clear and adequate. Those gifts for signs were of all consequence in their place; but how could a tongue or a miracle perfect a saint? We see, in the first Epistle to the Corinthians, that, instead of perfecting, they on the contrary became a very great snare for the saints. No doubt the Corinthians were carnal, and therefore they were like children amused with a new toy—with that which was, indeed, an engine of power. And we know how great a danger this is, just in proportion to our unspirituality. We have the very solemn lesson, that even the greatest powers and most astounding manifestations of the Holy Ghost in man cannot give spirituality, and do not minister to the edification of the saints necessarily in any way; but, if there be a carnal mind, they become a positive means of the soul exalting itself, turning away from the Lord, losing its balance, and bringing discredit upon that which bears the name of Christ on the earth. In this Epistle, however, God is occupied with His counsels of grace in Christ for the church, beginning primarily with the saints as such. He always takes up the question of individuals before He deals with the church. And how blessed and wise is this! He does not begin with the body of Christ, and then end with the perfection of the saints. This would be, very likely, our thought, but it is very far from His. He first puts forward the perfecting of the saints, and then shows us the work of the ministry, and the edifying the body of Christ. Thus, the true explanation of the passage is, that it is the development of Christ's love to the Church. His eye is fixed upon the blessing of souls. It is Christ not only gathering in, but building up—causing them to grow up to Him in all things. Accordingly, He gives the gifts which are of grace suited to this end. "He gave some apostles and some prophets."

These are the two gifts which the second chapter of this epistle shows to be at the foundation, we may say, of this new building, the church of God. Thus, in the 20th verse, we read, "They were built upon the foundation of the apostles and prophets, Jesus Christ Himself being the chief corner stone." Evangelists, evidently, are not the foundation; neither are pastors and teachers; but prophets, as well as apostles, are. And we can easily understand this. We can see that, as God was introducing into the world a wholly new system when He set His Son at His own right hand—a new work of God in the church, so there was a new word which had to accompany this work, whereby He would act upon the saints so as to give them to grow up to the perfecting of His will and the glory of His Son in this unprecedented thing, the church of God. Accordingly then we have the foundation laid, and here not Christ alone. Of course He is, in the greatest and highest sense, the foundation— "Upon this rock I will build my church": the confession of His own name, His own glory as the Son of the living God, is this unquestionably. But still, as the means not only of revealing the mind of God touching the church, but also particularly of laying down with authority the landmarks of His husbandry in the earth—the church of God, the apostles and prophets were thus used. To distinguish them the former were characterized by an authority in action, the prophets by giving out according to God His mind and will about this great mystery.

It is hardly worth while to disprove the notion that the prophets here refer to the Old Testament. The phrase "apostles and prophets" is strictly limited to those that followed Christ. Had there been the inverse order—prophets and apostles, there might have been some shadow of reason for this idea; but the Spirit of God, in His wisdom, has taken care to exclude the thought. The work spoken of is altogether new. The apostles and prophets seem to be expressly introduced in this order. But in the third chapter a decisive reason is furnished by the Holy Ghost. It is written in the 5th verse that the mystery of Christ, "which in other ages was not made known unto the sons of men, is now revealed unto His holy apostles and prophets by the Spirit"; so that we have there with the most perfect clearness not only the same order still preserved, but the positive expression "*now* revealed". The prophets of the Old Testament, therefore, are necessarily excluded. These prophets are of the New Testament as well as the apostles.

But more than this, let me make the remark before going farther, that this character of ministry was altogether new. When our Lord was upon earth, no doubt there was more or less preparative action for it. He sent out first twelve apostles; then He sent out seventy to carry a final message to His people. All this was a thing never found in any age previously. It was wholly without precedent on the earth—an activity of love that went out with a blessing to others. God Himself had not done it; for the solemn word by a prophet, and the secret action of His grace before, are too distinct to be confounded with it. Who had ever seen or heard such a thing as a Man on earth gathering men to Himself first, and sending out from Himself afterwards a message of love, the glad tidings (not yet, of course, in the fulness which was afterwards imparted when the great work of redemption was done, but at any rate the blessed news) of the King on God's part of the kingdom of heaven on the earth? This is what the Lord did on earth: He sent out disciples or apostles with the message of the kingdom. And no doubt it was in man's eyes a strange and to faith a blessed thing, suitable only to Him who had divine grace as well as divine authority, worthy of and reserved for the Lord Jesus here below. But it is remarkable that in Ephesians 4 all the earthly part of our Lord's action is left completely out, and the gifts here spoken of are beyond controversy dated from the ascension of the Lord, and shown to hinge on it.

Do I mean to deny that the apostles were included—the twelve, or, strictly speaking, the eleven along with the one supplied to fill the place of him that was cut off? In no wise; but nevertheless their earthly call and mission are quite passed by. We can all understand that the Lord as Messiah might prepare a mission suited to Israel, as I have no doubt that "the twelve" had this distinctly as its reference; for the twelve apostles naturally answer to the twelve tribes. The sitting on twelve thrones, spoken of in connexion with them also in Matthew 20, clearly confirms the thought. What hinders these same men afterwards from becoming the vessels of a heavenly gift?

Thus we can recognize in the earlier apostles a sort of double relationship. There was a link with Israel which was conferred by the Lord when He was upon earth in the midst of His people, dealing with them; but a new place became theirs when the Lord ascended on high.

But besides the Lord took care to break in upon this Israelitish form and order, and the apostleship of St. Paul becomes an event of cardinal importance in the development of the ways of God, because therein all thought of Jerusalem, all reference to the tribes of Israel, is dropped, and that takes its place which is clearly extraordinary in all its circumstances and heavenly in source and character. More particularly this was plain, that the Lord made manifest what was really true with regard to the others, that they on the day of Pentecost received that gift of apostleship which was suited to the heavenly work which they were afterwards to have, in addition to their previous earthly call and work. Apart from and towering over the twelve stood the apostle Paul, bringing out into the utmost prominence the principle that his apostolic mission was a heavenly thing, entirely and exclusively such as far as he was concerned. Therefore he was the fitted person to say, as it was of course by the Spirit of God that he did say, "Though we have known Christ after the flesh, yet now henceforth know we him no more." The glory of the Messiah on the earth fades away for the time in a deeper and brighter glory, the heavenly glory of Him who is now at the right hand of God. It is the same Christ, the same blessed One, without doubt, but it is not the same glory; and more than this, it is a better and more enduring glory. It is the glory that is suited to the new work of God in His Church, because it is the glory of its Head. "Now is the Son of man glorified, and God is glorified in him. If

God be glorified in him, God shall also glorify him in himself, and shall straightway glorify him."

Thus, the church being a heavenly body, and Christ Himself, its Head, being in the actual and fullest sense a heavenly person, ministry takes a heavenly shape: and these gifts which flow from Him are its first expression. Hence, then, we have the clear intimation from the scripture before us that these gifts from Christ on high are heavenly in their character and source.

Another thing also may be noticed by the way. If we take the bestowal of these gifts as dating from the ascension of Christ, where is there room left for the hand of man? Where can you insert that preliminary ceremonial on which tradition lays so much stress? Who ordained the apostles for their heavenly work? Who laid hands upon them, as authoritatively installing them in that high office? You will say that unquestionably the Lord called them when He was here "in the days of His flesh". He did call them for their mission to Israel; and when risen, but still on earth, He charged them to disciple the nations (Matthew 10; 28). But what hands of man did He employ in setting them apart to their proper heavenly work? Will any believer breathe the thought that this was an imperfection in their case? Did the new work of God, based on a dead and risen and ascended Saviour, and carried on by the Holy Ghost sent down from heaven, want anything for its due commencement? If there is no appearance then of that rite of laying on of hands, which some count not merely desirable, but essential for all that minister from the highest to the lowest grade, how comes this strange omission? Who will venture to impeach the regimen of Christ? Will any zealots for "holy orders", as men speak, affirm or insin-uate that the Lord did not know better than they what became His own glory in His chief ministers? Let them beware of their theories and their practice, if either lead them to become "judges of evil thoughts".

In truth, the Lord took care, now that it was a question of a new and heavenly testimony, not absolutely to abolish that ancient sign of blessing, but to break in upon and leave no excuse for the earthly order so easily abused by man. Hence, as if for the purpose of manifesting yet more distinctly the vast change which was come in the case of him who styles himself emphatically "minister of the church" (Colossians 1), there is no derivation from the twelve apostles that were before him. On the contrary, from His own place in heavenly glory the Lord calls one who was not going up to Jerusalem but rather from it; one who had no connexion with the apostles—nay, so much their enemy, that most stood in doubt of him, after he was arrested by sovereign grace in the midst of his determined systematic hatred of Christianity and persecution of all who bore the name of Jesus. What a proof that not only the conversion of Saul of Tarsus was of the pure and rich mercy of God, but that his apostolate sprang from the same source and bore the same stamp as the salvation which reached him! Thenceforward he becomes the characteristic symbol, as he was the most distinct and abundant testimony, of the grace that is now not saving only but choosing vessels and fitting them as instruments for the active blessing of mankind, and especially of the church of God. It was the Lord Jesus at the right hand of God calling and sending an apostle to the church, a chosen vessel unto Himself, to bear His name before the Gentiles and kings and the children of Israel; but first taken out from both Jew and Gentile and then sent to them (Acts 26:17).

The same principle embraced the other apostles no doubt: because they on the day of Pentecost were made gifts of grace in the highest degree to the church from the now ascended Lord, its Head. But there is fresh and brighter light in the case of Paul, who was not more truly "as one born out of due time", compared with all those that went before, than he furnishes in the strongest colours the unmistakable intimation of the mind and will of the Lord as to the future.

But then it will be objected that after all there was a miracle in Paul's conversion and call, which takes the case out of just application to ordinary ministry. A miracle most striking and significant there was, when the Lord in glory revealed Himself as the Jesus he was persecuting in the members of His body. Notwithstanding it rested mainly on the apostle's testimony; and there were not wanting, even in the church of God and among his own converts, it would seem, those who questioned the apostleship of Paul. His call far from Jerusalem, his isolation from the other apostles, the very fulness of grace manifested toward him, the emphatic heavenly stamp imprinted on his conversion and testimony, all tended to make the case peculiar and irregular and unaccountable, wherever the old earthly order so prevailed as to cast suspicion on any display of the Lord's ways beyond or different from the past. Personally a stranger to the Lord during His manifestation here below, there was no question of his candidateship, like a Joseph or a Matthias, on the ground of his having companied with the twelve from the baptism of John till the ascension. There was no decision by lot in his instance, nor any formal numbering with the twelve. He was a witness of Christ's resurrection no less than the rest, yet it was from no sight of Him after His passion upon earth. He had seen the Lord, but it was in heaven. His was the gospel of the *glory* of Christ no less than of God's grace. Thus carefully was the great apostle made the witness of non-succession, that is of a ministry direct from the Lord independently of man! No doubt the highest expression of that ministry was in Paul, who thenceforward becomes the most illustrious exemplar of its source and character.

Allow me also to put another question. Who ordained the prophets of the New Testament? when and how and by whom were they appointed? who ever heard of hands being laid upon their heads? Search the New Testament through, if you wish the best proof that the notion is unfounded. Let me come to the point at once, and affirm further, that neither prophets nor any other of these classes were installed of man after that fashion. Here we have apostles, prophets, evangelists, pastors and teachers: can you show me a single instance among these classes where the individual was called by human authority? Is it denied then that there was such a form of blessing as the laying on of hands in the New Testament? For my part, I accept the fact not only in its apostolic application to the sick and to those who had not yet received the Spirit, but also in its connexion with our subject. The question is as to its scriptural use? Let me ask, When were hands ever laid on any save to confer a gift by the power of the Spirit, or to commend those already gifted to God's grace in a special work, or formally to assign men to the charge of secular work? It is clear, for example, that Philip, along with his six companions, had hands laid upon him; but was it for his work as preaching the gospel? On the contrary, he was one of the seven men chosen "to serve the tables", in order that the apostles might not be distracted from

167

prayer and the ministry of the word. "The seven" thereon were ordained to be employed in the external service of the church. Apart from this, the Lord was pleased to send him forth in the proclamation of the word here and there; as an evangelist naturally would be a wanderer, not according to the meaning of the word so much as the exigencies of the work.

Hence, when the persecution about Stephen broke out and scattered those in Jerusalem, Philip had a new task which had nothing to do with his local duties as one of the seven. His diaconal service would station him at Jerusalem, to take care of the poor, for this was the purpose for which he was ordained; whereas his preaching Christ flowed from a gift of that character, not from ordination. In fact as far as the New Testament speaks— and it speaks fully and precisely—*no one was ever ordained by man to preach the gospel.* Hands were laid by the apostles upon Philip like the rest, after he was chosen by the multitude, and thus he was appointed to take charge of the tables; for the scripture, perhaps because of a certain peculiar state of things at Jerusalem, does not positively give the title of "deacon" in this case, though one does not deny its general justice, for there was something akin in their duties.

It is certain therefore that whether we look at an apostle, or a prophet, or an evangelist, or a pastor and teacher, or either of these last, there was no such ministry instituted for the church, which itself existed not, until after our Lord's ascension; and in none of these cases was there the laying on of hands as the initiatory sign or inauguration of these ministers. All admit the imposition of hands in certain cases, ordinary or exceptional. The exaggeration of clericalism should not hinder the Christian from being perfectly fair in dealing with this and every other question. There is nothing that will dispose of prevalent traditions so readily and conclusively as searching and submitting to scripture. There is full and clear instruction there, the effect of which is to confute all that tends to exalt man and lower Christ, whatever support men may try to extract from the word of God for selfish ends. It is outside the light of inspiration that all these errors live; once let that in, and it will soon be seen that the Holy Ghost is not providing for the worldly honour of man on earth, but for glorifying Christ in heaven.

What, then, is the genuine meaning and scope of Acts 13? It has long been the well-known stock passage which theological controversialists are wont to cite for ordination in general. Some insist on it as warranting their "three orders" of bishops, priests, and deacons; others allege it as decisive for parity of ministers, whether Presbyterian or Congregational. The Episcopalian points with triumph to Barnabas and Paul in the first rank; to Simeon, Lucius, and Manaen in the second; and to Mark in the third (as, after the dispute with Barnabas, to Paul, Silas, and Timothy respectively).[6]

Only examine the passage, and the more closely you do so, the better will you be enabled to judge how little it countenances, how strongly it condemns, every scheme of ordination which men attempt to base upon it.

In the church that was at Antioch there were, it is said, "certain prophets and teachers, as Barnabas, and Simeon that was called Niger, and Lucius of Cyrene, and Manaen, who had been brought up with Herod the tetrarch and Saul." That is, we have these five prophets and teachers, while engaged in serving the Lord with fasting, made the object of an important communication from the Holy Ghost respecting two of their number. "Separate me Barnabas and Saul for the work whereunto I have called them." Barnabas had been for years actively engaged in the work of the Lord; and so had Saul of Tarsus ever since his conversion. Not only was he set apart in the providential purpose of God before his birth, as we see in Galatians 1, but he was called by the grace of God from the time when he was struck down on the way to Damascus. But the Spirit of God now separates him to a special mission. It is clear that this is not an announcement of the ministerial call of either Barnabas or Saul: scripture is arrayed against scripture by all who say so. The previous part of the Acts proves that Barnabas was long blessed in the ministry of the word within and without, and that Saul especially was bold and mighty in the work. The latter, indeed, from the first, brought out the Sonship of Christ in a way which we have no reason to believe any other had done up to that time, as we learn from that very chapter which gives us his conversion. The notion therefore that ordination was the question in Acts 13 is most manifestly false.

But how comes it that the theologians fail to notice that their determination to see ordination here destroys their respective systems, as well as contradicts other scriptures? Who was it ordained Paul and Barnabas, and to what? These are called apostles in the very next chapter (14:4); and hence evidently the notion of ordaining Paul and Barnabas is quite unfounded, unless those whom God has set second and third in the church can ordain the first (1 Corinthians 12:28). Again, the truth is that there is not the smallest reason to call Mark a deacon at that time. He accompanied them as their "minister" (probably to get lodgings, to invite people to come and hear the word, and in general to serve them on their missionary tour); but, as for his being their chaplain, it is mere illusion. John Mark preaching to Paul and Barnabas! The truth is that he then turned out an indifferent help in the work, because he soon tired and went home to his friends. However this only by the way.

But it is transparent, that those who turn the account into the ordination of Paul and Barnabas involve the consequence that it is actually the inferior class conferring the highest ministerial rank upon them! If they were not apostles before, they have nothing to allege in support of the dignity but the sandy foundation that the act of laying on of hands upon them at Antioch conferred the apostolate! In this case it was an equal, if not a lower grade, giving a higher rank to those above themselves. Thus, it is evident that the notion is altogether unfounded.

Is it insinuated then that there was no meaning or value in this laying on of hands? That would be indeed to treat the word of God unwarrantably. It was a solemn and precious act of fellowship with these honoured servants of Christ. It was an act not only valid then but valid now. But there was no pretence of conferring anything whatever. The real drift of the transaction is expressed in chapter 14:26. It is said, that they "sailed to Antioch, from whence they had been recommended to the grace of God for the work which they fulfilled." Such was the aim of the laying on of hands by their companions in labour at Antioch; for it may not have been the brethren generally, but only those engaged in the work, and I wish to make every concession that is fair to those who desire to draw the utmost from the passage. But the meaning of the act is neither more nor less than a sign of blessing or of fellowship with those going forth on their new missionary errand. It was probably repeated. (See Acts 15:40.)

The laying on of hands was of the most ancient date in the Old Testament. Thus Genesis gives it in the case of a father or grandfather laying his hands on the children; and so in the New Testament we have the frequent use of it where there was no pretence of conferring any ministerial character. It was a sign of recommendation to God by one who was conscious of being so near to God that he could count upon His blessing. The Lord takes up little children, lays His hands upon them, and blesses them; and so with the sick too when healing some. It was not at all a question of ecclesiastical order in these instances. No doubt there were cases where hands were laid on for the purpose of inaugurating an office.

It is often thought that the same rite was used in instituting elders, as in Acts 14:22-23, where the apostles Barnabas and Paul were "confirming the souls of the disciples, and exhorting them to continue in the faith, and that we must, through much tribulation, enter into the kingdom of God. And when they had ordained them elders in every church, and had prayed with fasting, they commended them to the Lord, on whom they believed." But this is an assumption. It is not exactly said here or anywhere else that hands were laid upon the presbyters. This silence, if the fact were so, is remarkable. It may have been probably the case; but scripture takes care never to say it. We have the statement that hands were laid upon deacons. We know that an elder was a much more important personage in the church than a deacon. People may reason and speculate; but I have no doubt that the Spirit of God, seeing the superstition that was attached to the form of laying on of hands, took care never to connect the two things together in a positive manner. The passage which some conceive does so is in the first Epistle to Timothy (5:22), where Paul tells him to "lay hands suddenly on no man". But the object of this is too vague for a sure conclusion, the connexion being by no means certain. There is no allusion to elders expressly after verses 17-19. Thus in the 21st verse we read, "I charge thee before God and the Lord Jesus Christ, and the elect angels, that thou observe these things, without preferring one before another, doing nothing by partiality." How can one suppose elders in particular referred to there? I see a general description of his work in verses 20, 21, after which comes the exhortation on which so much has been built—"Lay hands suddenly on no man, neither be partaker of other men's sins." It is possible that there may be included in this an allusion to the danger of haste and carelessness in accrediting an elder, but the language is so comprehensive as to take in, it seems to me, every case which might call for the imposition of hands.[7]

But supposing that it did certainly refer to elders and that hands were laid on these functionaries as well as on deacons, the important and undeniable fact in scripture is, that elders were never ordained except by persons duly authorized, who had a real commission from the Lord for the purpose. Now many may imagine that this is a concession fatal to the free recognition and exercise of gifts. They may think it yet more strange to find that those who contend for the largeness of the action of the Holy Ghost lay the utmost stress upon a divine commission and a definite authority. But be assured that the two things go together, where they are held according to God. None will be found to be more tenacious of godly order than the very persons who plead most for the rights of the Holy Ghost in the church. My assertion is, that in this very matter of ordination Christendom has missed God's mind and will, and is ignorantly but not without sin fighting for an order of its own, which is mere disorder before God. If scripture is to decide, the common plan of ordination for all who minister to those without and within is a departure from the order of God prescribed in His word.

Undoubtedly in the case of "the seven" (Acts 6) you do find apostolic appointment. The great point in this case was, that there the congregation elected and the apostles solemnly appointed. But it was no more than the congregation choosing fit persons to take care of their poor, &c. Nothing could be more proper. It shows the condescending goodness of God towards those who gave of their substance and those who received it. If the church contribute, it is according to His will that the Church should have a voice in the selection of those in whom they have just confidence that they will distribute in God's sight not only with good conscience and feeling but wisely. Thus one sees here a conspicuous instance of God's wise and gracious care. The multitude chose such men as they deemed most suited to the exigency. But even here the mere choice of the believers did not give them that place in itself; for if all chose, none but the apostles appointed them over the business, secular as it was.

The principle tells in a directly opposite way with regard to the elders, and yet more as to the ministerial gifts of Christ. We have no such thought expressed as a congregation choosing elders—never in any part of scripture. On the contrary we have the fact that the apostles went about; and where assemblies were already formed, in which were persons possessed of certain spiritual and moral qualifications which pointed them out to their spiritual and experienced eyes as suitable for eldership, such they chose. Among these antecedents those who desired the office must be persons of good report, and who, if married, had only one wife. There were many individuals brought to the faith of Christ in those days who had several wives. This was a scandal and sure to be felt the more as Christian truth spread. Such a direction showed what was in the mind of God. One could not rightly refuse the confession of a man who had two or three wives, if he were converted; but he must not expect to become an elder or bishop; he could not be a suitable local representative of the church of God.

Again take the case of a man who had children brought up badly. Perhaps this neglect may have been before he was converted; perhaps after conversion he may have entertained the evil notion of leaving the children to themselves on the faithless plea that God, if He saw fit, would convert them some time or other. Such mistakes have been made, and miserable have been the results. Whatever the cause of an unruly house, its head could not be a bishop. No matter what might be his spiritual gifts, they could not countervail; no such man could be charged with the oversight of God's assembly. For such an office it was not so much a question of gifts as of moral weight. A man might be a prophet, a teacher, an evangelist—his disorderly wife or children would not nullify his gifts; but he ought not to be made an elder, unless he brought up his children with godliness and gravity, and himself walked with a good report among those without.

Thus the Lord stringently required in such an official these moral qualifications as well as spiritual capacity for his work. Even if one possessed all these things, he was not an elder because he had them unless duly authorized. He needed to be ordained; he must have a legitimate appointment besides. And in what did this consist? Manifestly the whole value turns upon a valid appointing power. In what consisted that competent authority? Are we to set up or to imagine one? It must be according to the Lord and His word. Now the Scripture allows of no valid appointing power except an apostle or an envoy who had from an apostle a special commission for the purpose.

Where is there such a delegate now that can produce an adequate (that is, an apostolic) commission for the work of ordaining? You never saw, neither do I ever expect to see, the like. The fact is, that the word of God nowhere hints at the continuance of an ordaining power. It demonstrates in the most explicit manner that, after the Lord set up churches here and there, when He established local functionaries in each church, apostolic appointment or choice and this only was what He stamped with His approval. The requisite qualifications are clearly laid down; but the fact is equally clear that none but an apostle or an apostolic delegate was warranted to nominate the elders to their office, and *not a word about perpetuating that power of appointment after the apostles left the earth*. We have an apostle writing, not to the church or churches to choose elders, but to one who was specially charged to do this task. Yet even to Titus there is not a word about another continuing the task; nay, not a hint that Titus himself was to continue it after the apostle was dead. Neither was Titus authorized to appoint where he pleased, but the apostle assigns him the sphere of his commission. Being a special envoy of the apostle, Titus was doubtless a teacher and preacher. But here there was a definite region where he had the duty of ordaining elders in every city. Titus was responsible to do this in Crete; but nothing is said of the establishment of elders elsewhere or at other times nor of his permanent continuance there. On the contrary—and this would be a strange direction for a diocesan—he was to be diligent to come to the apostle at Nicopolis. He was not to be left at Crete.

It is evident that such directions as these from the apostle to Titus afford no warrant for others to appoint elders now. This is pure assumption, whereas all depends on a valid authority. Titus was apostolically commissioned and could produce an inspired letter of instructions to him personally. Who can to-day do anything analogous? "It must be so" is a poor and vain reason to him who respects due authority. It is easy to settle matters after a sort where this is allowed to pass; but, beloved friends, we want the word of God. Let me ask for a plain answer to the question, Do you believe that the word is perfect? Do you doubt whether the Lord, who cares for His own order in the church, did or did not foresee all the need and difficulty? Do you insinuate that He forgot anything of real value to us now? Do you suppose that He omitted to take into account the death of the apostles? He did nothing of the kind. The apostle speaks distinctly of his death (and more than one apostle too). He speaks of perilous times and the importance of scripture after he was gone; but not a thought about a line of successors to appoint afterwards, not a hint about bequeathing his powers in this case. To you who are commended to God and the word of His grace, to you who tremble at His word, is that silence nothing? To my own mind it is a fact not more surprising at the first blush than increasingly pregnant with meaning the more it is weighed.

Popery, despising this fact, assumes the contrary from human reason and is built upon this contrariety. Not that one cares to denounce any one system in particular by name, save only to bring out the truth which shows the will of the Lord and proves the evil by the good. In truth every earthly system, no matter how opposed it may become to the word of God, begins by adding something of its own to that word. The power of ordination attaches not to bishops but to apostles and their delegates. The moment you allow men the principle of development after the scripture canon closed, the moment you clothe with apostolic authority a body of officials who never were authorized divinely for the work undertaken, you are off the ground of faith in and deference to the word of God. The present practice has not the smallest foundation in scripture.

Indeed one may safely go farther and affirm not only that the ordination, of which people talk so much, before preaching and teaching Christ, is not a thing to be coveted in the present shape in which it is found among men, but that it is now a disorderly institution, a grievous dishonour to the Lord who gives ministerial gifts by the Spirit. In short it is a mere and sorry imitation of what is recorded in the word of God. Examine well, and you will soon find it does not even resemble what we read of there. God's word remains true, sure, and plain: only there once was a positive personal commission, armed with a certain apostolic authority either direct or indirect; and this you ought to have if you pretend to ordain elders as Titus did.

Permit me now to press another question. Which is the most scriptural course—to do what was always becoming in a Christian, or to copy an apostolic delegate? Which commends itself most to your conscience, to your heart, to your faith? We will suppose now in this place an assembly of God's children. They see in the word of God that, beside the common privileges and duties of all saints, there were certain gifts for ministry, and that there were also certain offices which needed an apostle or his representative to fill them up. They would like to have them all of course; but what is to be done? Are they to neglect what was written to the assembly at Corinth or to the saints at Ephesus, and to ape what was not written to the church but to Timothy or Titus? Would it not be humbler to consult the word of God and inquire of Him, that they might learn what is His will concerning this matter? What do we see there? That as to the gifts of Christ they never required any sanction here below before their exercise; nay, they never admitted of human intervention. The only exception is where there was a positive power of the Holy Ghost conveyed by the laying on of the apostle's hands. Fully do I admit that there was an exception in such circumstances. Timothy was designated by prophecies beforehand for the work to which the Lord called him. (Compare Acts 13:1-2.) Guided by prophecy (1 Timothy 4:14; 2 Timothy 1:6), the apostle lays his hands upon Timothy and conveys to him a direct power (χάρισμα) by the Holy Ghost, suited to this special service he had to accomplish. Along with the apostle, the elders who were in the place joined in the laying on of their hands. But there is a difference in the expression the Spirit of God employs, which shows that the communication of the gift depended for effective agency not in any way on the elders but only the apostle. The particle of *association*

179

($\mu\varepsilon\tau\grave{\alpha}$) appears where the presbytery are spoken of, that of *instrumental means*[8] ($\delta\iota\grave{\alpha}$) where the apostle speaks of himself. It was an apostle that communicated such a gift. Never do we hear of elders thus conferring a gift: it was not an episcopal function but an apostolic prerogative, either to communicate spiritual powers or to clothe men authoritatively with a charge. Hence it is admitted that in the peculiar case of Timothy there was by the laying on of apostolic hands a very special effect produced; but who can do this now? Were this the claim (however one might desire to view, not indifferently but with the patience of God, the prevalent and superstitious perversion of a sign, admirable in itself when applied and understood scripturally), yet if any man now presumed to convey a spiritual power like an apostle, should one hesitate to call him an impostor? A mistaken course in assuming the rights of an earthly sovereign is or may be treason. What is it to pretend falsely to communicate the Holy Ghost or a distinct power of the Holy Ghost in the name of the Lord?

Beloved friends, it is a grave thing to trifle thus with the Spirit of God. There are those in our day whose ignorant boldness fears not to arrogate the right of conveying the Holy Ghost and ministerial power in this manner; but, thanks be to God, they are otherwise known to be fundamentally unsound, so that their influence over the faithful is inconsiderable. Then we have alas! the Eastern and Western bodies of Christendom, which are hardly less guilty. But among ordinary Protestants and especially among men of average Christian respectability, such pretensions are regarded with pity or horror. Even where the formularies as in the Anglican Communion approach fearfully near the precipice, the excuse is that their godly framers intended no more than to impart fitting and scriptural solemnity to various offices in the church. I admit however, that the excuse is lame, and that it is hard to decide whether these most suffer in conscience who employ these very serious forms ecclesiastically without believing them, or those are most injured in faith who accept as divine pretensions which are doubtless more respectably connected and venerable but not better founded than those of a modern imposture.

But the important truth on this subject to be seen is that these ministerial gifts were given by the Lord without any form further than that He warranted and sent them. Beware of disputing His will and wisdom. How is one to judge of the possession of a gift? Undoubtedly by its due exercise which finds an answer in the conscience. Let me ask you again, How do you know a Christian? When people talk theoretically, or discuss polemically, there are always great and numerous difficulties in the way. But if you went for practical reasons to a godly clergyman or dissenting minister, he could give you ample means of judging who are Christians in what he calls his flock. Listen to many a man on his knees and, if he be a Christian, he will speak as a child to his God and Father; but hear him on his legs, and he will perhaps controvert, without knowing it, what he has been just saying in prayer, till on his perverse principle he cannot tell whether God is his Father or not. How happy that there are such seasons of devotion where people speak with simple-hearted truthfulness! Away from their systems let them speak to God, and their true characters and even condition will soon be manifest as a general rule. Thus the fact is that in practice Christians have little difficulty in knowing for the most part who are converted and who are not. There may be a certain number of doubtful souls of whom we need not speak now. Let a believer be sent for to a sick man; is he wholly at a loss how to speak? Does he not seek as soon as possible to gather whether the sick man has peace in Christ, or is anxious about his soul, or whether he has ever realized his lost and guilty condition? If the believer finds no sense of sin, he will solemnly warn of judgment and set before that soul the cross, imploring him to receive Christ; or he will exhort him to rest in Christ because he is assured of his faith.

If then so little haze really rests on the question who are and who are not children of God, think you that the possession of a gift is a question so obscure and doubtful? Some may have more gift than others. But the gift of teaching implies the power of bringing out the word of God and applying it aright. Again take the power of ruling—for there is such a thing as rule in the church, and I hope none here present imagine it is gone—he who has the gift of rule seeks to exercise it of course according to the word of God. Scripture knows nothing of a blind obedience. The conscience is awakened, the heart set free and attracted to Christ. To these is the appeal of Christian ministry. It is not the blind leading the blind, nor is it the seeing leading the blind, but rather the seeing leading the seeing. Christ gives liberty as well as life, and this withal responsible to do the will of God. Therefore it is that according to the intention of God His children do not well to contrive systems to escape difficulties; they need faith to go through them with God. Let them prove their gifts, if indeed they have gifts from the Lord, by real power. There may be severe trials and difficulties now and then. Even Paul himself had to do with doubters of his apostleship, and this within the church, and among his own children in the faith. What true-hearted man should be downcast if *he* is slighted? But the time came when the Lord vindicated His servant, and when the self-will and pride which refused a divine gift was utterly put to shame, if the heart was not brought back to lowly thankfulness. The chief mistake we are apt to make is in the way of impatience; we do not allow time and space for the Lord to work: and that lack of patient waiting only defers the wished-for solution, because it makes the difficulty so much the greater.

But as to the discernment of a ministerial gift for preaching or teaching, it is in general plain and simple. If a brother stand up to speak in the Christian assembly without a gift from God, he will soon and painfully find it out. If self-judging, he will learn much from his own conscience; but he may quite sufficiently soon hear from others that which will make him understand that he has not a gift in the judgment of his brethren. But where there is really a gift, is it not possible that prejudice may act, and this be refused? Certainly it may be so for a time. Perhaps the speaker thinks too highly of his gift; perhaps he mistakes the character of it, and the right scene and time for its exercise; perhaps he is too exclusively occupied with his line of things, and too urgent or anxious to assert his gift. All this may be, often is, and always creates difficulty. But the truth remains that what is of God approves itself in the long run. My own experience, as far as my limited range of observation and knowledge goes, inclines me to think that the children of God are prone to make too much rather than too little of gift. In the present state of the church there is but a feeble development of gift, and this is felt the more in proportion to spiritual intelligence and a true position. Do you wish to know your place fairly and fully? Look in confidence to God and search the word of His grace. Many things there are to hinder and to draw away: partly the effect of education, partly the difficulty of finding an honest livelihood, especially if a man has been a professional preacher. If he abandons (not preaching but) that profession as an unscriptural innovation, he for the most part loses everything, even his bread, unless he have private means of his own. Hence it is that the inducements for such an one to remain where he is are enormous; the difficulties of coming out at the word of the Lord are incalculable. The power of God alone can accomplish the change and sustain the soul in peace and praise, "steadfast, immoveable, always abounding in the work of the Lord."

While we may be sure that the word and Spirit of God give us clearly the true position for the individual Christian and for the Christian assembly, we ought not (I think, as things are,) to expect a great variety and strength in the gifts of the Lord's grace. Of course He can work sovereignly, and assuredly we ought to be most thankful for what is given. No doubt also there are gifts distributed somewhere or other. There are gifts of Christ in members and ministers of the national establishments, I do not question; there are His gifts likewise in the dissenting societies; and are we to suppose there are none of His gifts of grace in Romanism itself? For my part I cannot doubt that there are. Who would, who could, reject the testimony of facts that there have been persons therein—such as Martin Boos, for instance, not very long ago—used for the conversion of sinners and for the helping on of saints in some degree? And are such men not gifts of Christ to the church—as truly gifts though in the false position as if they were out of it? Their being Romanists—ay, Romish priests—does not destroy His grace, whatever we may feel as to their faithfulness. The fact is that the Lord gives according to His own will by the Holy Ghost, and we ought to acknowledge these gifts wherever they are. If a man be a dissenter, whether a minister or one of the people, in either case I am satisfied he is in a false position. It is not a question of a feeling of dislike to dissent, if one believe its foundations to be unscriptural. I ask the forbearance of any dissenters who may be here in affirming calmly and solemnly my conviction that dissent is unsound in its distinctive principles; a thorough contradiction of the very character of the church as one body; and in the popular call and choice undermining ministry as a divine and permanent institution flowing from the Saviour's grace. Dissent is religious radicalism, which essentially opposes God's will as much as and perhaps more than any other principle. The proofs are too plain. Dissent substitutes the election of the people in the place of the sovereign choice of the Lord Jesus Christ whether immediate or mediate.

But how is the truth better secured in the national bodies? By patronage, clerical, lay, or governmental! And the painful apology for this systematic self-will is that the men nominated by the government of the day, or a landlord, or a college, or a corporation, have gone through the usual forms! Is there the faintest resemblance between this worldly machinery and the divine system of spiritual gifts from Christ set forth in Ephesians 4? I see only One who has ascended up on high. Are you looking to any other person? to any other kind of ascent? to any other heaven for the favours you crave after? I appeal to you as Christians. Do you value the word of God? Do you cherish that word only for the salvation of your souls? or do you confide in the same word and Spirit for guidance as to ministry and church office? What subjects more simply belong to the Lord? For what do we need Him more? As a believer I surely feel the want of God's word for my daily walk, no matter what my circumstances or sphere or duties. And do you, can you believe that the word that lives and abides for ever does not concern itself with so grave, delicate, and spiritually needful a thing as the ministry of the word; or that, if it speak thereon, you are not bound to hear and bow?

The sum of what has been said is then that these two great principles are revealed in scripture and recognized by the early church: namely, the Lord giving gifts of His own grace which did not require human intervention; next also a system of authority which did require that intervention, as in the appointment of elders by the apostles or persons commissioned to do their work in certain cases. It is clear that we have neither apostles living on the earth, nor representatives, like Titus, charged by an apostle to do quasi-apostolic work. The consequence is, that now, if subject to the word of God, you cannot and do not look for elders in their precise official form. If any man allege these can be, it might be well to hear his grounds from Scripture. What has been produced is in my judgment amply sufficient to disprove it. You cannot have persons formally and duly appointed to this office, unless you have a power formally and duly authorized of the Lord to appoint them. But you have *not* that indispensably needful power to authenticate elders: this is your fatally weak point. You have neither apostles nor functionaries commissioned by the apostles to act in their stead; and therefore the entire system of appointment breaks down for want of competent authority. Dare you say of *your* elders that the HOLY

GHOST has made them bishops? You have none really, *i.e.*, scripturally entitled to appoint.

What then? Are there none suitable to be elders or bishops, if there were apostles to choose them? Thank God! there are not a few. You can hardly look into an assembly of His children without hearing of some grave elderly men who go after the wanderers, who warn the unruly, who comfort those that are cast down, who counsel, admonish, and guide souls. Are not these the men who might be elders, if there were a power existing to appoint them? And what is the duty of a Christian man as things now are in the use of what remains? I say not to call them elders, but surely to esteem them highly for their work's sake, and to love and acknowledge them as those who are over the rest of their brethren in the Lord. I ask you solemnly, beloved friends, do *you* acknowledge any to be over you in the Lord?—any living servants of the Lord to take the lead in Him? Do you imagine such a recognition as this an offence against the principles of God? Rather let me warn you against picking out certain favourite texts from God's word to which only you pay obeisance. If we do so, we are as far as in us lies building up a sect no less truly than our neighbours. On the other hand, beware of adopting that human invention—apostolic succession—to escape dilemmas. If under the fiction of succession we dare to call men apostles who are not, the Lord in due time will not fail to challenge our word or act, and demand, who entitled us to endorse such an unheard of thing as this? who gave us leave, without His word, virtually to acknowledge this or that as an apostolic man by accrediting his claim to ordain? It is evident that to ordain elders is, however well-meant, an imitation of what apostles did, and, if unauthorized, not only without validity but an unwitting usurpation of an authority which reverted and now pertains to the Lord Jesus Christ alone. Thus in the present state of the church, the difference between a true position and a false one is not at all that one has got a due ordination and the other wants it. In truth no body on earth possesses it now. Do you acknowledge the want? or are you trying to cover the humiliating but evident fact that you have not the only ordaining power which scripture sanctions? And yet you go on ordaining, though you have neither apostle nor apostolic deputy! Which course is most orderly? To do as you do; or to acknowledge our actual lack, and carry ourselves accordingly before God and man—to confess that we want apostles or their delegates, and therefore that we cannot have presbyters duly chosen and formally appointed? There are, I repeat, men endowed with such qualifications as would render them eligible, so far as we can pretend to say, *if* there were a competent ordaining power. And the general principle of Scripture (Romans 12) manifestly is, that he who had the gift of ruling, or of taking the lead among the saints, is bound to use it with diligence (as the teacher, exhorter, and others, are responsible to discharge their respective functions), even if circumstances made legitimate appointment to a charge impracticable.

But subjection to the word of God discovers readily that a state of things substantially analogous to our own defective condition is provided for in Scripture. The Lord in His wisdom let such wants be felt in the early church. Thus the apostle was inspired to write epistles to churches where there were no elders; as for instance the epistles to the Thessalonians and to the Corinthians. The last was notoriously a disorderly church, and elders might have been thought useful there. Nevertheless not the least word or hint about elders there is heard from first to last. Had elders been then in their midst, would not the apostle have called *them* to account, and blamed their want of godly care and diligence in oversight? Of this there is not a trace. Further, we know it was not the practice of the apostles to constitute elders in an infant church. Where Paul and Barnabas chose elders for the disciples, it was in assemblies that had existed probably for years, and thus there had been time for spiritual qualifications to be developed. But in a new assembly, where the saints were young comparatively, a certain time had to be allowed, so that those who were competent for such a work should be made evident. Accordingly it is rather a rare thing to read of the apostles choosing or appointing elders.

On the other hand, in the first epistle to the Thessalonians, we have in the last chapter very important instruction given to the saints. They, too, are a similar instance of a young church, yet they were told to own those that laboured among them. Hence all this may be where presbyters are not. Thus in 1 Thessalonians 5:12-13 the apostle writes, "We beseech you, brethren, to know them which labour among you, and are over you in the Lord, and admonish you; and to esteem them very highly in love for their work's sake." The presence of elders is not requisite in order to have and to own those who are over us in the Lord. There is much of importance for us now in that Scripture, for we have elders no more than they. I think we ought to lay its exhortations to heart. There are within and without, not a few ill-instructed souls who hold the notion that, unless there be official appointment, they cannot have anybody over them in the Lord. This is all a mistake. No doubt, when a man was officially appointed, there was a definite guarantee in the face of the church given by an apostle or an apostolic man; and there was thereby no little weight given to those who were thus appointed. Such a sanction had great and just value in the church, and would be of consequence among the unruly. But none the less did God know how to provide instruction for assemblies where there was not yet official oversight. How merciful for times when, for want of apostles, there could be no elders! But it will be noticed that the Corinthian assembly abounded in gift, though elders are seen nowhere among them. The Thessalonians do not appear to have possessed the same variety of out-ward power, while elders or bishops again are never hinted at. Yet at Corinth the household of Stephanas devoted themselves regularly (ἔταξαν) to the service of the saints; and the apostle beseeches the brethren to submit themselves to such, and to every one that helped and laboured. The Thessalonians he prays to know those who laboured among them, and presided in the Lord, and admonished them. Evidently this did not depend upon their being apostolically appointed, which could hardly have been in their circumstances as lately gathered. It is founded upon that which after all is intrinsically better, if we must be content with one bless-ing out of two. Surely, if it comes to be a question between real spiritual power and outward office, no Christian ought to hesitate between them. To have the power and the office combined is no doubt the best of all, when the Lord is pleased to give both; but in those early days we see that individuals were often and rightly engaged in the work of the Lord before there could be the seal of an apostle, as it were, affixed; and such the apostle encourages and commends earnestly to the love and esteem of the saints before and independently of that seal. How precious that we can fall back on this principle now!

Even at Corinth and Thessalonica then those were raised up in the midst of the saints who showed spiritual ability in guiding and directing others. That was the work of those to whom one epistle exhorted subjection, and whom the other epistle commended as "over them in the Lord". Such men as these did not labour only; because some might be actively engaged in the Lord's work who might not be over others in the Lord. But these manifested power to meet difficulties in the church, and to battle with that which was ensnaring souls, and so to guide and encourage the weak and baffle the efforts of the enemy. They were not afraid to trust the Lord in times of trial and danger, and therefore the Lord used them, giving them power to discern and courage to act upon what they did discern. This was part of what fitted them to take the lead in the Lord. There were such at Thessalonica as well as at Corinth, and yet there is not the slightest intimation that they were regularly installed as elders, but on the contrary the strongest evidence that elders as yet had not been constituted in either place. The regular practice was to appoint elders after a certain time; indeed it could only be when the apostles came round, or sent an authorized delegate to choose fit persons and clothe them with a title before the church which none but the bad would dispute.

Need I observe how God had been graciously providing for the wants of His children? This subject will come definitely before us on the next occasion on which it will be my lot to address you. I will not therefore do more now than draw attention to His far-reaching wisdom in meeting the difficulties of the day, when a valid authority to ordain as the apostles did is not left on the earth. Not that His children are left without help; they have the same Lord and the same ever-present Spirit. Hence there is no need of some change or new invention to meet the difficulties of the day, but the return in faith to what was and is the will of the Lord; and this with intelligence of the actual state of the church, and the feelings which become it.

We have seen that, as the rule, the Lord alone gave these gifts of ministry: it depends upon His love to His church, His faithfulness to the saints. Is the Lord Jesus one whit less tender and true now than He was on the day of Pentecost? Who would insinuate it? Neither can I sympathize with those who look wistfully back on the earliest times, as if they only afforded scope for faithful souls. No doubt a bright halo of grace surrounds the scene where the Holy Ghost was first poured out on men with a simplicity and power which carried all along; but who was the spring and whence the energy which produced fruits so much the more wondrous when we think of the soil once so hard, and stubborn, and cold? Was it not the Lord acting for His own name by the Holy Ghost after He took the place, in risen and ascended glory, of giving gifts to men? Is not His grace as equal to these perilous times as He proved Himself when ushering in the mystery that was hid from ages? Are there saints to be perfected and ministerial work to be done? Does the body of Christ need to be built up? Then assuredly His gifts cannot fail till the work is done and all are brought into the unity of the faith; and the many adversaries and subtle snares and increasing perils will only draw the more upon the faithful love of the Lord of all. There is fulness of blessing in Christ for the church now as truly as then. Would that we but confided in Him more for every exigency!

Are we then to disparage the truth or to doubt His grace by setting up some work of our hands, some calf of gold, as if we knew not what is become of Him who is gone on high? Far be it from God's children! Let me suppose you come together as God's assembly; you know not who is to speak, exhort, give thanks, pray. To unbelief this is but confusion. Certainly it looks unwise if I forget who is in the midst; it is unpromising if I do not believe that the Lord is there; but if assured that He, who has all power in heaven and on earth, loves and cherishes the church, and that the Holy Ghost, divine as He is, dwells with and in us, what need I fear? If this position is true for one saint, it is true for all. For my part I would not dare for a moment to stand upon any foundation which did not contemplate the whole length and breadth of the church of God, which did not in its faith and love go out to and embrace all the saints of God. Of course allowance must be made for exceptional states, as for persons guilty of sin that would require their exclusion (immorality, bad doctrine, and such like).

But then if I know that this *is* the ground of the church according to Scripture, and that there was no other from the first taken and acted on by the holy apostles, the question is, Am I upon it? If I am called to labour in the word and doctrine, the Lord points me out the way. He opens the door which none can shut, He shuts and none can open. He finds a path for the feeblest of His pilgrims, and gives them courage, and makes it plain if they have to serve Him. Let us never doubt Him.

But may there not be a number of gifts? So much the better. If there are five or twice five gifted men in an assembly, let us thank the Lord: there is room for all. God forbid that we should sanction the novelty of each minister having his own little flock! Is it not a degradation for those who so speak, and for those so spoken of? No one behaves himself—nay, he does not even know how to behave himself—who does not bear the sense in his soul that the saints are "the flock of God". But evidently men do not speak of God's flock, if the divine ground of the church be forgotten: then it is "my flock", or "your flock". There is always room for the exercise of His gifts, whatever and however many they may be. Besides it is a strange time to fear that any could be spared as superfluous.

The hour warns me that this subject must now be closed. My endeavour has been to expound and enforce the fundamental distinction between gifts and offices— the one, we saw, flowing from Christ on high, the other requiring appointment here below of men themselves authorized of the Lord for the purpose. As for gifts, they always remain sure as truly as Christ abides the head and source of supply. As for formal authorization, it is no longer possible because you have not a duly authorized power to appoint. All you can do in the direction of appointing, if you will do something, is to set up a paltry and rather arrogant imitation of the apostles and their delegates. But if you really love the Lord and value godly order, is it not your bounden duty in the name of the Lord to acknowledge all His gifts in a way you have never done? Acknowledge them privately and publicly in the work He has assigned them. If the gift be small, acknowledge the Lord in it as heartily as if it were a great one; and if it be a great one, acknowledge it as humbly and unjealously as a small one. On the other hand do not try to imitate what the apostles did; beware of pretending to do what ought not to be thought of unless there were apostolic power. And as to appointing deacons or choosing elders, scripture affords no warrant unless there was direct or indirect apostolic authority which does not now exist.

NOTE ON ACTS 14:23

This opportunity is taken to furnish clear and conclusive evidence against the notion that the elders were chosen by the votes of the churches. The word χειροτονέω, if etymologically viewed, means to stretch out the hand; hence it was applied to election, as we say by show of hands, and, generally, to choice or appointment without reference to the manner. Just so ψηφίζομαι starts from mere reckoning with pebbles, and was used for voting thus; then for voting in general, and lastly for the simple resolve or decision of the mind. The context, not the word in itself, shows which is to be understood. Hesychius explains χειροτονεῖν by καθιστᾷν (compare Titus 1:5), ψηφίζειν; as Suidas for χειροτονήσαντες gives ἐκλεξάμενοι. With all this accords the usage of Aristophanes, as well as of Æschines, Demosthenes, &c., both in the narrow and literal sense, and in the general meaning of choice or designation. Appian, Dio Cassius, Plutarch, Lucian, and Libanius afford many examples where the word conveys no more than choosing. In these therefore the idea of popular suffrage with or without the hands stretched out is quite excluded.

But a few instances must be given from Hellenistic writers familiar with the Old Testament and contemporaneous with those inspired to write the New Testament. Thus Philo (περὶ Ἰωσὴφ [On Joseph]) repeat-

195

edly uses χειροτονέω of Pharaoh's appointing Joseph his prime minister, and of Moses in the place to which he was chosen by God, and in his selection again of Aaron's sons for the priesthood. So Josephus (*Ant[iquities of the Jews]* Book 6, chapter 13 § 9) speaks of Saul as "chosen king by God", ὑπὸ τοῦ Θεοῦ κεχειροτονημένον βασιλέα, and also (*Ant[iquities of the Jews]* Book 13, chapter 2 § 2) represents Alexander as writing to Jonathan in these terms, χειροτονοῦμεν δέ σε σήμερον ἀρχιερέα τῶν Ἰουδαίων. "We constitute thee this day high priest of the Jews." This may suffice to prove what we are to judge of Dr. J. Owen's statement (*Works*, vol. 15. pp. 495, 496, Goold's edition) that "Paul and Barnabas are said to ordain elders in the churches by their election and suffrage; for the word there used will admit of no other sense, however it be ambiguously expressed in our translation." Indeed, Beza, Diodati, Martin, and others had committed themselves to the same thing. Dr. G. Campbell, however, Presbyterian as he was, repudiated this version of the text, and (in his *Prelim[inary] Diss[ertations and Notes, Critical and Explanatory]* Dissertation 10, Part 5 § 7) pronounced *per suffragia* in the Latin of Beza "a mere interpolation for the sake of answering a particular purpose". If one do not endorse so strong a censure, the only alternative is that the gloss sprang from inadequate research and strong prejudice.

The truth is that we need not go beyond the New Testament to demonstrate the error; for here as elsewhere, even when applied to the most rigid election, χειροτονέω never means choosing by the votes *of others*, which it must mean to bear the alleged sense. Wherever the word occurs technically, the person intended does not take the votes of others merely, or preside as moderator of the election, but *is the voter himself.* Now in this case the subject in question is beyond doubt not the disciples but Paul and Barnabas. If any voted by stretching out their hands, it was the apostles only. Hence the authorized version rightly dropped "by election", the sense given in some of the older English and foreign translations which had been too much influenced by the Genevese school and even Erasmus.

The true meaning is that the apostles *chose* elders *for* the disciples in each assembly (not the disciples for themselves). And this is entirely confirmed by Acts 10:41 and 2 Corinthians 8:19; in one of which passages God is said to have chosen beforehand; in the other the churches are the choosers precisely as here the apostles. Neither God nor the assemblies gathered the votes of others: no more did Paul and Barnabas. But this is the sole testimony which has ever been imagined directly to favour the popular election of elders; and we have seen that the inference drawn is assuredly fictitious. For the matter in hand the usage of the word in the political or civil affairs of Greece is no evidence.

It is perhaps hardly necessary to add that χειροτονέω does not mean the imposition of hands, for which scripture supplies another phrase never confounded with the word in question. But this confusion soon began to show itself in ecclesiastical authors, who not infrequently employ χειροτονία where we might expect χειροθεσία or ἡ ἐπίθεσίς τῶν χειρῶν. This error occurs in the so-called Apostolical Canons, Chrysostom, and subsequent writers; and it may have led the authorized translators to give "ordained" rather than "chose" or "designated". Bishop Bilson, in his "Perpetual Government of Christ's Church", is guilty not of this confusion only but of the strange error that "the elders" included "deacons". (See chapters 7 and 10.) But really the discord of commentators is almost past belief, unless one have read extensively and proved the fact by experience. Thus Hammond tries to extract from this verse the appointment of a single bishop to each church or city; whereas one might have inferred (without appealing to such incontestible proof to the contrary as Acts 20:17, 28) that the plurality of the presbyters with the singular distributive was as strongly against him as language could make the case short of an express contradiction. Had Hammond's idea been meant, nothing could have been easier than to have written πρεσβύτερον κατ᾽ ἐκκλησίαν or πρεσβυτέρους κατ᾽ ἐκκλησίας. On the other hand, if I may trust Mr. Elsley's report, Whitby opposes this ultra-Episcopalianism on the equally untenable ground that these elders were such as had miraculous endowments either directly from God (as in Acts 2, 4, 9, 10, 11) or through an apostolic medium (as in Acts 8), and who had the care at first of the churches; not fixed ministers, but nearer to the apostles in rank. Can any statement be conceived more random and unfounded?

The last and perhaps the worst specimen of this speculation I take from Calvin's Inst[itutes] Book 4, chapter 3 §§ 15, 16, where, according to the author, "Luke relates that Barnabas and Paul ordained elders throughout the churches; but he at the same time marks the plan or mode when he says it was done by suffrage. The words are χειροτονήσαντες πρεσβυτέρους κατ᾽ ἐκκλησίαν (Acts 14:23). They therefore selected *(creabant)* two; but *the whole body,* as was the custom of the Greeks in elections, *declared by a show of hands which of the two they wished to have."* It has rarely been my lot to meet with a more glaring perversion of the facts and language of inspiration than this passage exhibits, the refutation of which has been already anticipated. The new translation by H[enry] Beveridge is purposely cited to cut off cavil on that score; and the original is given underneath for verification.[9] It is consolatory however to find that so untoward a construction was destined to no long existence; for its own author smothers it though with reluctance in his commentary on the passage:— *"Presbyterium* qui hic collectivum nomen esse putant, pro collegio presbyterorum positum, recte sentiunt meo judicio" *(Comment. in loc. [Commentary on Timothy, Titus, Philemon (1 Timothy 4:14)]).*

But the close of the chapter is still more full of perplexity and error. "Lastly it is to be observed, that it was not the whole people, but only the pastors who laid hands on ministers, though it is uncertain whether or not several always laid their hands. It is certain that in the case of the deacons it was done by Paul and Barnabas, and some few others (Acts 6:6; 13:3). But in another place Paul mentions that he himself without any others laid hands on Timothy. 'Wherefore I put thee in remembrance that thou stir up the gift of God, which is in thee by the putting on of my hands' (2 Timothy 1:6). For what is said in the epistle of the *laying on of the hands of the presbytery* I do not understand, as if Paul were speaking of the college of elders. By the expression I understand the ordination itself (!); as if he had said, Act so, that the gift which you received by the laying on of hands, when I made you a presbyter (!), may not be in vain." That apostolic hands appointed the seven men whom the multitude elected for the service of tables is clear. But scripture is silent whether imposition of hands was practised in the establishing of elders; and to me that silence seems admirably wise, even if in fact hands were imposed, as a divine provision against superstitious abuse. But what can be meant by the reference to Acts 13:3, connected with the allegation that Paul and Barnabas, &c., laid their hands on deacons? As for the notion that τοῦ πρεσβυτερίου (1 Timothy 4:14) means not the elders as a body but eldership, and so is to be in sense dislocated from its evident and necessary connection with χειρῶν at the end of the verse and put in apposition with χαρίσματος at the beginning, I maintain that the grammar is not more harsh and unexampled than the resulting doctrine is strange. Eldership in scripture is not a gift but a local charge.

The modern defences of this system are of no more weight than those of older date. I have before me now Dr. Crawford's "Presbyterianism Defended", and Mr Witherow's Inquiry; but they seem to me neither candid nor successful. The insuperable difficulty is that presbyters in scripture were never the ordaining power, though they might be associated with an apostle even in conveying an extraordinary gift as to Timothy, who is never represented as an elder. Further, *the* minister is as distinct from the elders in Presbyterianism as he is from the deacons in Congregationalism, and is a personage of as high moment in both systems as he is unknown to scripture. Again, to say that elders are not as distinctly laymen as the minister is clerical among Presbyterians is inconsistent with the notorious difference as to style of address, and salary. Both their systems err in maintaining that the office-bearers were chosen by the people; only those were whose duty it was to disburse funds or its equivalent. And if there was a plurality of elders (who were identical with the bishops), there was the fullest opening for all the gifts of the Lord, instead of that invention of men, *the* minister. Elders never ordained elders, but only apostles or their delegates; and gifted men required no ordination before exercising their ministry. Nor does Acts 15 resemble a church-court, *i.e.* a representative assembly of ministers and elders from all parts of the sphere of jurisdiction. This scripture shows us the apostles with universal authority from Christ, and the elders of the Church in Jerusalem, with the whole Church joining in the decision. Hence the decrees were delivered to be observed far beyond the cities of Jerusalem and Antioch, in total discord with Presbyterianism.

Lecture 6:
The Resource of the Faithful in the Ruins of Christendom

2 TIMOTHY 2:11-22

How many elements of solemnity are crowded into the subject now before us! It is solemn to look over Christendom and survey its ruins, now too palpable to be denied. It is solemn, on the other side, to think of the faithful goodness of God, who knew all beforehand, spread it out in the unerring word of His grace, and has shown us that, if He felt the evil that was about to cover the scene of the profession of Christ's name on earth, His loving wisdom descried a sure path—a path the vulture's eye does not see, which nevertheless He gives His people to discern, and by means of which they can have the happy certainty that they are pleasing God.

To those who for the sake of the Lord and the truth deplore and refuse to have fellowship with the current practice of Christendom, there may be a certain necessity to give as strong proofs as may be of those evils which now abound, and of which the word of God forewarned when they were but in the germ. Indeed there may be a kind of temptation to prove the evil, where we feel in anywise the need of a justification for the path of separation to God. But that tendency is corrected promptly, and the heart receives its due tone and its right attitude, when we think who after all is most concerned, and whose honour it is we have to justify. The Lord preserve us from thinking of ourselves! It is unworthy of those who belong to Christ. Be it our boast to justify Him alone.

It will be my business now to show, not that He needs aught from us, not that His words of light require the tapers of man to make them more distinct, but that divine charity seeks the blessing of every one, especially of those who are comparatively young and uninformed in the truth of God. I hope to give enough at least of the evidence to show most plainly what the will of the Lord is; how faithfully His word deals with us; how worthy of trust both He Himself is and that which He has put into our hands. This may encourage the most diffident of God's children to look up with confidence, seeing that the end was as plain to Him as the beginning, and that for us the only path is that of Christ, for there cannot be two. He is *the* way, and as there is but one Christ, so there can be therefore but one path that satisfies the heart and mind of Christ for those who love Him.

Am I going to produce strong reasons as if one needed to justify this? It will be enough to explain what He has pointed out. To those who know Him there will be the most complete justification and the strongest reason in the fact that it is His path for us, though His goodness has given, alas! too sure and abundant proof how deeply it is needed.

Further I shall have the opportunity to-night of slightly reviewing the ground over which we have passed on previous occasions, and of showing how all that is most precious has been secured to the faithful. Not that the Lord has not been pleased to take away much. Not that we ought to be unfeeling about anything that concerns the Lord's power and glory in the church. But if we rightly claim a higher place for that which concerns God in His moral ways; if we ought to feel that what brings and keeps before us the grace of Christ must be of deeper value than any displays of power before men; yet on the other hand, beloved brethren, it would be a wrong to the Lord if we looked with cold indifference on the utter weakness of this our day, and the dishonour thus put upon the name of Jesus in Christendom itself. Alas! there is no place among the outside strangers to the Lord Jesus where there is more daring enormity done than in the very scene where men are baptized in His name. When we look back at times long past, at the early days of the church's pilgrimage on the earth, and the power of the Holy Ghost then displayed, I am persuaded we ought to feel for the wounds inflicted in the house of His friends; we ought to be grieved that the bearing of the church was such that the Lord could not outwardly pour honour upon her, but was obliged to strip her as it were, and shame her before the enemies of His name.

Let us own all this, as also the far deeper sorrow that men so little prize the truth, so tamely feel for the honour of the Lord's person in Christendom, not to speak of the well-nigh universal want of feeling even what the church is in its barest and simplest forms, and still more the total forgetfulness of its bright portion as one with the Saviour, and of that which the church hopes for in the day to come. Be assured that if we do not thus feel with the Lord in our little measure, we are not in a moral condition rightly to act upon His word in present things. It is a lesson of no small importance to see that the Lord has not given us in scripture that which admits of bare imitation. It does not suffice to take up the epistles of St. Paul for instance, and set to work as if we were competent to put in order the things that are wanting, and ordain elders here or there. It is one thing to fall back upon the word God has given us, and quite another to assume that we can reinstate the church now that it has been broken up and ruined. It is right to feel its low estate, but that we should now build up again that which is thus fallen the very thought proves that the heart in this has no communion with Christ; that there is a lack of due holy distrust of self; that there is such insensibility to the true state of things now as unfits not merely for authoritatively restoring the church, but even for the humbleness of faith that confides in the actual resources of Christ. For it is an unvarying principle of God, that when there has been a departure from Himself, it matters not under what circumstances or time or place or people—whether before the flood or since—whether in Israel or in the church—God insists upon it that the first step in that which is morally good should be the sense of our real evil in His sight. When this is the case, the presumption will be far from us that *we* can make good that wonderful display of divine power, grace, and wisdom—the church of GOD! It was the greatest work, so to speak, that God ever wrought upon the earth (next to the Cross, whereby alone such a work became possible).

God forbid that in thinking of what He has done, we should compare that which stands alone—alone throughout all eternity! But if we look at all that has ever been done upon the earth, or even the very making of heaven and earth, I say, that the work of God in His church—the church of God—was greater still. And now, we poor leaky vessels that could not keep the blessing, we that have been through our own weakness and unwatchfulness a prey to Satan's wiles, and let in the thieves and robbers that have spoiled the house of God, are we the men to set it up again? Is this the feeling of lowly faith? If it were bad for man to go away, if it were a grievous thing for Israel to dishonour the law of God, what must it be for the church to slight God the Holy Ghost? It is the epistle of Christ, the habitation of God through the Spirit, the object of His most perfect love, accepted in the Beloved, even in Christ, made the righteousness of God in Him. What is it then for that church practically to forego the glory of God here below—to prefer the work of their own hands to His word and Spirit—once more to bow down to idols graven by art and man's device? Oh! it is more loathsome than that which scripture or even history records of days and men infinitely less privileged.

Think not that I am exaggerating what Christendom has done or does. Nor do I wish to dilate more than is absolutely needful upon the painful failure of that which bears the name of Christ here below. In truth it is not so. But let us hear what the word of God says upon the subject. Who would allow the thought that He speaks too strongly of that which He saw from the first, and told us was coming as He looked into the future?

Let us begin with the Saviour Himself and see what He intimated to His disciples should be found when He returns again to the earth, when He summons man to give an account of himself. In Luke 17 He tells us not that the world should become gradually changed from a wilderness to a Paradise, nor that the heathen should lay aside their false gods and the Jews their enmity to the true Messiah. On the contrary He gives the disciples the needed warning, that it was to be as in the days of Noah, and in the days of Lot. These were times of ease and worldliness, when all mankind was rising up against God; and yet they furnished comparisons for the scenes which are to meet the Lord as He appears from heaven to judge the world. "As it was in the days of Noe, so shall it be also in the days of the Son of man. They did eat, they drank, they married wives, they were given in marriage, until the day that Noe entered into the ark, and the flood came and destroyed them all." The self-security and love of ease will be substantially the same when the Lord is revealed as just before the flood. Then as of old men will be engrossed in the ordinary matters of daily life. Spite of the law, spite of the gospel, again is seen and will be continued that state of corruption and violence which brought the Deluge upon the earth no less guilty than utterly unconcerned. And Christ looks onward to the day of His return: no previous millennium of holy bliss awaiting Him; no happy rejoicing hearts characterizing the world generally then; but on the contrary the same moral condition, the same indifference to God's will and glory which preceded the flood.

After the flood when nations and tongues began there was another scene more appalling and degrading, which the same book of Genesis brings before us; and this also furnishes its sad complement to the picture of the days just before the Son of man comes again. "Like also as it was in the days of Lot; they did eat, they drank, they bought, they sold, they planted, they builded; but the same day that Lot went out of Sodom" (most ominous words!) "it rained fire and brimstone from heaven and destroyed them all. Even thus shall it be in the day when the Son of man is revealed."

If we take up now the Epistles, we shall find the light shed by the Holy Ghost in no way weakens but confirms in every respect the testimony of the Lord Jesus; only that now we have naturally the Holy Ghost looking rather at professing Christendom, whereas our Lord made the Jews His starting-point and centre.

Thus in Romans 11, without dwelling at length upon the chapter, the Spirit of God anticipates the end of Christendom. "Boast not against the branches. But if thou boast, thou bearest not the root, but the root thee." Such is the warning given to the Gentile professor. The Jews are meant by the natural branches. They had been the depositaries of promise of old, and had therefore the responsible place of testimony for God upon the earth. Hence they were the original branches of the olive tree, the line of promise and testimony on the earth which began with Abraham. But the Jews broke the law, went after idols, refused and slew the Messiah. There was a resource in the gospel; but they refused the gospel from heaven, as well as the Lord their King on earth. The consequence is, that the natural branches of the olive tree were broken off, and the wild olive, or Gentile, grafted into the old stock of profession. And this is the warning that is given: "Thou wilt say then, The branches were broken off, that I might be graffed in." Has not this exactly been the feeling of Christendom? Contempt for the Jews, astonishment at their wickedness, utter insensibility as to their own condition. "Well; because of unbelief, they were broken off, and thou standest by faith. Be not high-minded, but fear; for if God spared not the natural branches, take heed lest He also spare not thee. Behold therefore the goodness and severity of

God: on them which fell, severity; but towards thee, goodness, if thou continue in His goodness."

Let me ask any man that has the smallest fear of God, or even outward acquaintance with His word, Has Christianity continued in the goodness of God? Is there any Protestant, any Roman Catholic, who thinks so? Is there any person, no matter where, no matter who—a single soul who dares to say that Christendom, the professing Gentile, has continued in the goodness of God? The Romanist cannot think the Protestant schism continues in the goodness of God. The Protestant is assured that the Romish body is the fruit of clean departure from God in superstition; and so we might run through all existing systems. They may each plead for his own association; but who will say that even his own has continued faithful? They may believe that it means well, and would be admirable if carried out; but who would not acknowledge that it has not been carried out? that consequently no sect, no portion, no fragment even, has continued in the goodness of God? All agree that, as for the mass of profession outside themselves, it has failed to testify for the goodness of God. Consequently there rises up from men on every side the acknowledgment that the Gentile has not continued in it. Not that the failure is felt as it should be; not that there is adequate confession and renunciation of our common sin before God. Where sin is really spread out to God, it will not be persisted in. But at least there is an outward acknowledgment to a certain extent in the earth now, and quite enough to prove that Christianity has not continued in the goodness of God. What then says the word of the Lord? "Thou also shalt be cut off." The Gentile shall be cut off for his faithlessness, as surely as the Jew was.

This, remark, is not in some prophetic portion of God's word, which some might think ambiguous, though we do not allow the thought for a moment that any part of the word of God is so. But here in an epistle which every Christian allows to be one of the most fundamental and comprehensive, which takes up Christianity from its elements, and through which the Lord has established souls in peace, perhaps more than through any other portion of His word; it is in this epistle to the Romans that we have the solemn announcement of the sure cutting off of the Gentiles. Not merely one part or another but the Gentile profession is doomed of God, because it has not continued in His goodness; as truly as the Jew is now cast out from his heritage, a bye-word and a reproach to all the earth, evidently bearing his doom stamped upon his brow.

To examine many of the epistles would more than occupy my time. Suffice it to say, that as we travel down the stream from 2 Thessalonians, which was one of the earliest epistles written by Paul, to the latest, the Epistles of John and Jude, we have only an increasing testimony, growing more distinct and urgent and awful. As the evil grew, so the signs of judgment became more apparent. The Spirit of God sounds the trumpet with no uncertain note, and wakes up the faithful where there is an ear to hear. Christendom was gradually being undermined, and would become, in no long time, the engine of opposition to God—would be made the theatre of the grossest evil, taking up the abominations not only of the Jews but of the heathen themselves, and consecrating a system of Idolatry under the name of Christ and His mother, saints and angels, even more frightful and guilty than anything ever before found here below. For the very fact of praying to Peter, Paul, or the Virgin, proves that the light of Christianity must in some measure have been known, before it ended in so distressing an apostasy. Does any one think the expression "apostasy" over-strong? Allow me to tell them that the very phrase "the apostasy" is the expression of the Holy Ghost in the second epistle to the Thessalonians, where we are told "there is a mystery of iniquity which now worketh". Only there is now a hindering power. Consequently it would not burst out into its full development all at once; it was kept in check for a certain time by the good hand of the Lord for the purposes of His own grace. But the moment that this restraint was gone, then it would be no mystery any longer, but manifest lawlessness. It is called "a (or rather "the") falling away", or the apostasy. This must become ripe, and "the man of sin" must be revealed. Thus we have too plainly an uninterrupted succession of evil. This is the vista described in the scripture; a succession of evil that goes on always swelling in intensity and volume till at last when the restraint is removed, it bursts out into a yet more fearful issue—not "the apostasy" only, but "the man of sin". What a contrast to the Man of righteousness, when man dares to take the place of God in the temple of God!

This then is what Christendom is to the Christian watchman. It has not of course been realized in all its force, though I do not deny that there have been various and also growing manifestations of evil. As the apostle John tells us, "Even now there are many antichrists, whereby we know that it is the last time." This is so much the more remarkable because he shows that the Antichrist was coming, the great token of which is that there were many antichrists then. They knew thereby it was the last time. The Spirit would not close the volume of the New Testament until the worst evil was actually there at least in its germ; and this being so and descried by inspiration, there was need of nothing further. The Spirit of God could, as it were, fold up the sacred roll. It was complete. The mystery of lawlessness is shown already at work, "the man of sin" is predicted; the mystery of Christ and the Church no longer hid but disclosed. Scripture had attained its full compass. There remains, not some fresh view of Christ, so to speak, but contrariwise the unfolding of that Christ whom they had already, the bringing out more intimately and appreciatively the light of the love of God that was in the Lord Jesus Christ from the beginning. This is the antidote of all Satan can bring—to the many antichrists, and at last to *the* Antichrist. I refer to it in order to give a kind of connexion between the different states—the rise, progress, and final manifestation of lawlessness. Nay more the lawless one is to exalt himself against the Lord of glory. The last book of the New Testament shows the millennial reign over the earth, ushered in by the destruction of the beast and the false prophet with all their company, as Babylon had been previously destroyed.

Thus rapidly have we glanced without entering into all the proofs of the doom of Christendom. They are patent in the general epistles and in particular in the epistle of Jude where a most energetic sketch is given in the compass of a single verse (11). With that power which the Spirit of God only knows how to convey the shadows of Cain are sketched, then of Balaam, and finally of the gainsaying Core. Is there nothing for Christendom there? Is there no sound of sure if slumbering judgment there? "Woe unto them! for they have gone in the way of Cain"—that unnatural brother, that pretender to religion, who brought his offering to the Lord but slew the guiltless. Is there no presage in him who received the wages of unrighteousness—in the man who, spite of himself, prophesied glorious things of a people that he loved not but would have sold to destruction? Is there no solemn lesson in the wages received for teaching, it may be, the glorious things of God, without heart for His people, still less any care or jealousy for His word, for His will, for His glory? Finally, in the fearful rebellion of Korah, "the gainsaying of Core", in those who had the ministry of the sanctuary, in the proud Levites who coveted and arrogated to themselves the place of Moses and Aaron (the apostle and the high priest of the Jewish profession), is there no awful warning there? Have you never heard of men professing to be servants of Christ, and yet pretending to be priests strictly, officially, and exclusively—assuming to be authoritative channels of divine pardon empowered on earth to absolve from guilt before God? I do not speak only of such as claim in their heathenish darkness to offer a sacrifice for the dead as well as the living. Assuredly one thinks not with bitterness about such things as these, but we may all stand aghast as we survey the facts realized in Christendom. If it be a prophecy, it is a prophecy fulfilled.

All this may suffice to show how little Christendom has continued in the goodness of God. Details are needless. The godliest members of the various religious societies would be the first to confess the failure of their own. God's controversy is not with one only but with all, though doubtless the proudest will meet with a peculiar judgment. It is evident also that the word of God leaves it not to human experience or to spiritual judgment to infer His thoughts of Christendom; He has pronounced upon it Himself. Hence it is not presumptuous, but on the contrary the part of humble faith to believe God in this. How good He is thus to cut off the fear of forming a judgment so stern! For now he that does not pronounce after the Lord is ignorant of his Master's mind, or is false to His will. He that would defend or justify Christendom does not, in effect, fear to give the Lord the lie. From the scriptures enough has been given to show that the man who can look on Christendom and vindicate what is around us ignorantly or wilfully slights all the instruction that the Holy Ghost has given on the subject. Undoubtedly this is strong; but it is the Lord's goodness which makes the owning of it now to be a matter of sympathy with Him, and not of a proud claim to superior light.

God's word is open to all. By it we are all bound to see as He sees. The Lord admits of no vain excuses that *we* cannot judge. The Spirit of God, who judges and discerns all things, dwells in every Christian. He that says he cannot judge Christendom virtually denies himself to be a spiritual man; but if we do judge that Christendom has fallen into these predicted evils one after another, and that what was then but budding is now bearing the most bitter and baneful fruit, I ask, are we to partake of it? Are we to be insensible to our own share of the common sin? If the Lord graciously imparts the strongest warning, are we to satisfy ourselves with that flimsiest and most profane of apologies, that when the Lord comes He will set it all right? Yes, but it will be too late to set right my conscious Christ-dishonouring unfaithfulness; it will be to my shame to live till then indifferent to His word, careless of His glory, regardless of the Holy Ghost, who is grieved by that which I have been allowing practically. Am I, or am I not, to refrain from that which insults Him? If I know these things, am I to content myself without doing them. He who does puts himself in the guiltiest place of all. Do I know and feel the despite Christendom does and I have done to the Spirit of grace? Then let me look up in dependence on the Lord, that I may do it no more, nor settle down in a pretext so lame and criminal as that the Lord will set all to rights again. Is He not coming to judge every evil way? No doubt He will bring in good, and this from above! but He will judge all evil, and yet more than in times past. In vain then do I essay to shelter myself under the blessed truth, that the Lord is coming to display the kingdom of God upon earth. Assuredly, He will. From the heavens He will come, and fill the earth with the peace and blessing He brings with Himself, instead of finding it here below. A few poor broken hearts He will find in the world—a godly remnant, crying out, like the importunate widow in the guilty city where ruled the judge that feared neither God nor man. Such and worse will be the state of things, and in their midst shall He find faith on the earth? Yes, but crying out in alarm. And so He will clear the world with the avenging sword, before He establishes His throne of righteousness upon it. Of course I speak figuratively now; but the fact will be unsparing divine judgment; and therefore how blind for any to harden themselves in going on with sin under the plea that the Lord is coming to set the world and church to rights!

Allow me to say further, that the Lord has not left us to our own thoughts any more of the good than of the evil. He has given us His path, and this is what the heart desires to come to—the resources of the faithful in the ruins of Christendom. It were strange indeed if the word of God shed no sure light where it is so needed? Can we conceive such a thing as the Lord giving His view of the darkening future, and no provident care for His beloved and feeble and trembling followers? We began with the Lord's testimony about man's evil; let us see how He ensures good for His people in the midst of it. For Matthew 18 we may bless the Lord. Although He is giving instruction as to the animating spring of the assembly, which is grace, (as law was the governing principle of the synagogue,) the Lord provides what would be deeply needed, if they were reduced to a handful. "Where two or three are gathered together in my name, there am I in the midst of them" (verse 20). Could one conceive more tender thought, or more evident wisdom than the Lord thus caring for His own in a dark day? To this the goodly flock might come—that assembly which once stood out so fair, with its thousands on whom great grace rested. How wise thus to prepare the hearts of His servants! How well He knew and guarded against the anxieties of His saints! We know what numbers are to the worldly spirit, and how apt we are to rest upon that which looks great in the earth. Yet nothing is more destructive of Christianity. He that has not a heart for the two or three must be only a dead weight if he were among ten thousand. It might be no doubt that he would be carried along the stream of happy multitudes; and that which was thus unfaithful to the mind of Christ might pass unnoticed in the strong current and new-born delight in the Saviour, transporting all around, as was no doubt the case on that bright day when the Holy Ghost came down from heaven to be the herald of the glory of the Lord, and to make believing men on earth the dwelling-place of God. We can understand that at Pentecost the tide of joy rose so high as to cover all such elements, sure as they were to appear later on.

And soon it came, too soon, when sounds of discontent were heard even in that blessed habitation of God. Alas! man was there; not God only in His goodness but man; and behind was the adversary ready to dishonour the one through the other.

The church, like man and Israel, has to be tried on earth. What is the declared issue? Never was there such blessing entrusted to man; but man is as faithless under the gospel as he was rebellious under the law. The Holy Ghost is slighted as the Son had been; and in the day when eternal realities are revealed man turns back to the shadows of Judaism, preferring them to the substantial truth of God. This is the history of Christendom. And the Lord, with it all spread out before His prescient eyes, comforts His followers, were they ever so few and weak, with the assurance of His presence where His name has its central place to their faith.

In the prospect of coming evil how gracious of the Lord to think, it may be, of some obscure village—of some solitary ship that travels across the ocean—of some comparatively desert island—yea, or of the vast and crowded city, where the very solitariness of discipleship is more realized sometimes than anywhere else! Wherever, however, whenever it might be, the Lord gives His own weight of authority to the two or three gathered unto His name. It is not merely His blessing— where could He not bless? Blessing He went on high, and never since—if I may so say—never has He laid down the hands which He then lifted up in blessing. It could not be otherwise till He come in judgment. His work was infinite. Who could limit the preciousness of His blood? Who could say that redemption, like the first covenant, was grown old, and ready to vanish away? Could any difficulty, danger, or need in Christendom turn that grace back, as it were, into its spring, or dry up those rivers of living waters which they that believe should receive? It could not be; but there is more than all that here. Not only is there blessing but there is also the weight of His authority guaranteed to the smallest real representative of His assembly. We know that men shrink back from church discipline; and he need not wonder at this who is aware how it was made under the fairest pretences the most abominable scourge of tyranny the earth ever beheld. One cannot, therefore, be surprised that Christians who had escaped from the weight of that iron hand should somewhat shrink back at the bare sound. But we must beware of mistrusting Him to whom we owe our every blessing, because Babylon, the world-church, has perverted His words. But if there were only two or three, there ought to be as much jealousy as if there were three thousand to maintain publicly and privately, collectively and individually, ways consistent with the character of Christ. This cannot be unless there be discipline. The obligation of an united pure walk is bound up with the very integrity and being of God's assembly. It ceases to be the church of God, unless there be the holy earnest solemn carrying out of that which the Lord has laid down. "Purge out, therefore, the old leaven, that ye may be a new lump, as ye are unleavened." No ruin can touch this responsibility for a moment. On the other hand the Lord takes care in his grace that blessing shall flow spite of failure.

But there is more than the sovereign action of divine grace, where responsibility may have been little felt and the will of God misunderstood. The Lord watches over those gathered together to His name, and is there present in their midst were they but two or three. What unfailing and inestimable comfort! Conceive for a moment some Christian awakened to feel that the place of a believer is not to be a member merely of the ecclesiastical system of the country or of particular views, but on the contrary that the only thing which suits and is due to Christ is that we should renounce—we cannot be too lowly, but neither can we be too thorough in renouncing—every tie that is not connected with Christ. Where we can obey Christ in the midst of those that are His—where the Holy Ghost is allowed freedom to work according to the word of God—there is God's church, and nowhere else. The liberty of the Spirit is to exalt Christ and this only. This is a universal principle, true of an individual and true of the assembly. It would be a miserable thing if the assembly were not a scene of true and blessed liberty; but such it is that God may be glorified by Christ Jesus. There will be also the consciousness of that which is offensive just in proportion to the spiritual power that is in the assembly.

A great or a small company makes no essential difference. The Holy Ghost is sent down to care for the interests of the name of Christ. The two or three weak and ignorant ones gathered to it at least know that they are His; that they ought not therefore to belong to man; that they ought not therefore to be under any other tie; that rules made by one or many or all—if they were the very best that were ever produced—are not entitled to bind Christians, seeing that God has already furnished the only perfect standard not only of faith but of church fellowship, and that to own another is to dishonour the word of God and the Holy Ghost who is here to make it good in power. The question is not whether we can do better than others: God forbid: that indeed were presumption. But this I ask, whoever you may be (and I trust that, if you are a Christian, you will agree with me), Which is best, your rules or God's word? If God, and not you, be the wiser, how came you to invent these rules? You thought the word of God insufficient, and you must supply the deficiency! What is the result? Take what is going on at the present moment, and in any society you like. The very newspapers ring with the scandal of what is done under the name of Christ. What do your rules avail? Neither you nor the wisest of men can construct a standard for all time; and why should it be attempted? God has given His own, and His children need no other.

We have already the only sure and divine rule. The only want is the faith to value and act upon it. True, the consequences are serious. Faithfulness to Christ costs much now as ever. But is it not a solemn thought that now, in this boasted nineteenth century after the Lord has accomplished redemption, we are only awakening, here and there, to feel that the word of God is better than the word of man? What a discovery! Yet it is great as it is humbling that it should be a new thing—a discovery which many of the children of God have not yet made. All admit that God's word is infinitely wise for the soul's salvation. Who, when it is a question of eternal issues, would trust his soul to the doctrines of men? Then is felt the value of that word which reveals the Saviour, and of the blessed Spirit who makes the word precious in the revelation of Him. But is it not daring to draw these distinctions in the word of God, and to put aside that which speaks of the church, ministry, worship, the breaking of bread, and prayer? How comes it that men should behave practically as if God's word had less decision and authority in these matters than the shifting thoughts of man? How comes it that men so seldom think of being guided only by the word of God? How comes it that believers resort as a matter of course to human ecclesiastical rules? How comes it, for example, that dissenters, the best of them, when they want a minister in the word, proceed at once to elect him without a syllable of scripture for that course? Who gave them licence to do so?

"It must be so; we have our own doctor and our own lawyer, and why not our own minister?" It is exactly this worldly principle that has done the mischief. Why is not God consulted in His word? How comes it that in scripture a church never elects a minister? Of course there must have been many who wanted ministerial help in those days as now; and God, who knew all that is good, must have known every want also. How comes it that there was never a man chosen by a Christian congregation to preach the gospel or teach the saints—not a solitary instance in the word of God? They cannot get rid of the difficulty. What are they to do? The fact is, the dissenting principle is broken at the very outset. They cannot step over the threshold. They cannot do without a minister, and they cannot elect a minister according to scripture. Let us look now, not at congregationalism, but at the two or three gathered to the name of Christ. They too want help, these feeble ones; and what are they to do? This is the word of their Lord, "Where two or three are gathered together unto my name, there am I in the midst of them." God forbid that I should disparage the advantages of ministry; but to be simply subject to the Lord, whether or not He sends, is the best of all. The fact is, as we are not authorized, so we have no need to elect any; for all are ours already, "whether Paul, Apollos, or Cephas". It is for God to choose and give. He has bound up and made all His ministers part and parcel of the church. They are members of Christ's body. They are

His gifts to the church. It is ignorant and evil meddling for the church to elect. Besides, the moment you elect one to be peculiarly your minister, by that very act you defraud yourselves of all the rest. You are going out of the path of God in order to enrich yourselves in this respect; but that very act of selfish haste, like every other departure from the path of faith, brings, as the necessary result, the surest impoverishment. Suppose then people get their minister; he may be but young, and they may want to be nourished and fed up in truth. Unless he have all the gifts centred in his single person, they are reduced to his individual measure. Another again may be a pastor, and love the saints; but the congregation for the most part consists of persons needing to be converted, while he is not an evangelist but a pastor and perhaps a teacher. How evident that, if tested thus practically, man's ways always ruin God's work! The parochial system in the established bodies works as much or more evil. It may seem natural and prudent, but human wisdom in divine things is as foolish as it is fatal. What else could be expected by those who know God and man from a departure from the rich provision the Lord has made?

Let us now look on the other side. The Lord is there. The "two or three" do not exactly see their way. They are in presence of a great difficulty. Perhaps they have heard the whisper of some dreadful doctrine, and they do not understand it, not being versed in these matters. What then? They wait upon the Lord—a wholesome thing for any of us—most wholesome to be obliged to feel that the Lord alone can avail. But He does love and care for His saints. He raises up and opportunely sends a servant of His. The latent evil is brought out plainly; and the moment the light of God by whatever means is cast upon it, the conscience of the saints answers to the call of the Lord, and they repudiate it heartily for themselves.

Again there is one fallen into what may seem a little evil, yet enough to render him indifferent to the Lord, to His word, to His grace. He refuses to listen to the warning of one, then of more, and lastly of the assembly of God. "Let him be unto thee as a heathen man." He is not a heathen, but supposed to be a brother; yet he is treated as if he were a heathen, because he despises Christ in the church. This in fact is the case here supposed (Matthew 18). Such decision is trying to the heart, where will works among the saints. But it shows plainly that not their wisdom nor their experience guides aright, but the Lord in their midst; and He promises His presence if it were but two or three gathered to His name. Here then we have a clear and positive provision for the faithful in the worst of times. It is hardly possible to conceive of circumstances where there might not be "two or three".

It is well however to add that the essential point is their gathering to His name. It is not such a gathering unto Christ, where narrowness is allowed, or sectarianism, any more than in the grosser forms of letting in the world or tolerating evil. If any "two or three" were so happy together, as to look with suspicion on godly men outside them, they would forfeit their place of privilege, and be in a false position. Does the Lord so regard His disciples? Does He scrutinize them as if they were doubtful characters, or put them in quarantine as if the plague might be in them? I speak of saints where there is no suspicion of evil doctrine, direct or indirect, or of unholy walk. The Lord welcomes them, and so should we. His name has not its value where we are not large for His sake.

But there may be another case. A person comes of great repute in the world, who has been preaching and is universally respected; but alas! he betrays himself by a lack of heart and conscience where Christ is concerned. Him they refuse. Thus the same name of Christ, which is their warrant for welcoming the weakest that loves Him, is here exactly the same power for refusing the highest who does not love our Lord Jesus Christ in incorruption. What might is in that name to bring and keep together hearts otherwise alien, and yet withal what a delicate test for detecting and excluding what is not of God! If it be a question of truth, the name of the Lord is the only real touchstone; if it be a question of discipline, that name is strength to the feeblest heart; if it be a question between persons and principle, there only is found all needed wisdom and power both individually and as regards the assembly.

But let us look now at 2 Timothy 2. We have a picture drawn by the Holy Ghost of the professing body, the house of God. The first epistle duly cares for order and good government in the house of God. The second epistle anticipates the influx of evils to such an extent that the house is merely alluded to as a comparison. Still "the sure foundation of God standeth, having this seal"—on one side, "The Lord knoweth them that are His", and on the other, "Let every one that nameth the name of the Lord depart from iniquity". There are thus the sovereignty of the Lord on one side, and just responsibility on the other—two great principles which meet us everywhere. Then follows a more detailed application:—"But in a great house there are not only vessels of gold and of silver, but also of wood and of earth, and some to honour and some to dishonour." Some would take the place of knowing the Lord whom He did not own, and who felt not the incongruity of His name with iniquity. Timothy must be prepared for the development of evil among those that confess Christ—not only "some to honour" but "some to dishonour". "If a man therefore purge himself from these, he shall be a vessel unto honour, sanctified and meet for the Master's use, and prepared unto every good work." Separation from evil is the invariable principle of God, modified as to the manner of course by the special character of the dispensation. So Isaiah, Jeremiah, and the prophets generally. Is Christianity less stringent? It is now on the contrary that it becomes more urgent and absolute. "If a man purge himself from these [the vessels to dishonour], he shall be a vessel to honour." Put away the wicked (1 Corinthians 5); if this be no longer possible, purge yourself out from them. There is nothing man dreads and feels so deeply. You may protest, you may denounce, and it will be borne by the world as long as you walk with it in the main; but "he that departeth", now as ever, "maketh himself a prey". *Act* on your convictions, and the most honeyed courtesy turns sour; your desire to please God at all cost will be branded as pharisaical pride and exclusiveness. It matters not how gently and lovingly you purge yourself from the vessels to dishonour; the pain, the grievance, lies there, and nothing can sweeten it, above all in the eyes of those it condemns. Indeed it is more felt, the more graciously it is done, provided it be done thoroughly; for then evidently your motive is not disappointed feeling but desire to be wholly subject to Christ, with a heart perfectly happy in what they know nothing of and could not enjoy.

All this is an unpardonable affront in the world's eyes. Add to this, that separation is claimed in 2 Timothy from the religious or Christian world. "The Christian world"! what a phrase! what a contradiction! as if there could be the smallest possible alliance between Christianity, which is of heaven and Christ, and that outside world which crucified Him. No wonder that in this epistle we read of perilous times in the last days. What greater peril than, after they have known the truth, going back into substantially the same conditions of evil as were found in the heathen world before Christianity entered it. Compare 2 Timothy 3 with Romans 1. How painful the resemblance! The difference is, that some of the grosser characteristics of heathenism have been replaced by subtler evil. The comparison is most instructive. In this state of things the Christian profession is indeed a great house; and, as in such a house there is that which is destined to the basest uses, no less than what is for the best purposes, so in that great house which bears the name of Christ—if you please, "the Christian world".

If there, what ought you to do? It is a solemn question for the believer. He has no hesitation about the profane world; but the world bearing the name of Christ is a difficulty to him. Seeing that the Christian profession is there, am I not setting myself up and virtually condemning the excellent of the earth? But will you name any evil thing that has not had a good name attached to it? I do not speak now of such fatal poison as Socinianism or the like; but take Romanism, or the Greek church, or even sects known to be heretical, and yet by the malice of the enemy and the subtlety with which he has concealed his work some children of God have been entangled. It is too plain therefore that, whatever good men may do here or there, the only real inquiry is as to the will of the Lord. It is not a question of making others walk in your light, but you must *not* walk in their darkness. This is the great point, not occupying ourselves with others, prescribing what they must do, but feeling my own sin, as well as the common sin, yet by grace resolved at all costs to be where I can honour and obey the Lord. Is not this a true plain imperative duty, an undeniable principle of scripture, that commends itself to your conscience? It may be that you do not act accordingly; but you cannot deny that it is a right thing and what you ought to do.

But you are tied and have difficulties. Perhaps you have a family and friends you cannot bear to grieve; perhaps you have hopes for your children if not for yourself. Can a heart purified by faith thus set aside the Lord's word? Do you think He does not know your wants and does not feel for your family? You know the Lord loves yourself: cannot you trust Him for *a bit of bread?* You, who are trusting Him for eternal life and for heaven, cannot you trust Him to take care of you in the face of these trials and obstacles of every day? Perhaps you are too comfortable, too anxious about what is respectable for yourself and your children. Let the Lord deal with you; I am sure He will not harm you, but only do what is most loving and tender towards you and yours. Impossible for any heart to be beyond the Lord's love and wisdom and generous considerate care. If you really believe in Him, why not cleave to His word without compact or condition, and come forth at His bidding? You do not know what the next steps may be. It is enough that you know you are doing contrary to the word of God now. In vain we talk of loving, if we are not prepared to follow His word. Do you say you do not know what next to do? The Lord does not ask you: it is not His way to show all at once. Act on what you see from the word, and trust the Lord for what will follow; He is worthy of your confidence, and will give you more when you have taken the first step. But leave for ever that which is condemned in God's word. "Remember Lot's wife", and look not back, but go forth at His word wherever it points, and you will find that "whosoever hath, to him shall be given". And as regards the way, to the Lord rough or smooth is alike, deep or shallow, great or small; it may make a great difference to you, but the greatest difficulties only become the means of proving what the God is that we have found.

But there is more in 2 Timothy 2. Not only are you to separate, or purge yourself, from these vessels of dishonour, but the word is, "Flee also youthful lusts; but follow righteousness, faith, charity, peace, with them that call on the Lord out of a pure heart." Thus there is no excuse for isolation. Turn your back upon what you know is opposed to scripture. Have I to demonstrate to any Christian that what is unscriptural is unholy? Have I to urge that "to him that knoweth to do good, and doeth it not, to him it is sin"? If then you abandon what has no warrant from scripture, but on the contrary is condemned by it, hear this word of God: "Follow righteousness, faith, charity, peace." Follow them, not solitarily, but "with them that call on the Lord out of a pure heart". What consolation, even if there were but two or three! Are you afraid because there are only two or three? God may act on hundreds or thousands: this is a matter for Him. You are to follow the Lord's path through His word, with chastened spirit yet not sadly, but full of joy and thankfulness, if you find ever so few who call upon the Lord out of a pure heart. In other words, faith has a divine warrant to expect companions in its path, though it lie now through the ruin of the

Christian profession. As it is imperative to turn away from all known evil, and there can be no valid excuse for refusing God's call, so there is enjoined companionship in following after righteousness, faith, charity, and peace, with such as call upon the Lord out of a pure heart. May no hindrances nor dangers alarm, but knowing that it is the Lord who has thus graciously thought of us, may you and I and every one that loves that blessed name have unbroken confidence in Him! He addresses Himself to hearts grieved in the midst of dishonour to His grace and truth, and He has taken care to mark most distinctly the path not of separation only but of association—the path of departure from evil and of pursuing what is good.

How clearly the great moral principles of God remain in spite of disorder! How the operations of His grace survive all ruin! Thus the principle of the assembly of God abides in, it may be, only two or three gathered to the name of the Lord. Thousands of Christians, in a national system or in a dissenting sect, could not redeem their fundamental error; members of Christ may be in them, but the principle of God's assembly is abandoned in their very constitution. Let "two or three" come out at the word of the Lord, making His name their centre, and owning the Spirit of God as in and with them to guide them according to scripture; these, and these only, are carrying out His mind in the real intelligence of the Holy Ghost. It is no question of numbers, but of being gathered together, few or many, unto the name of the Lord.

All here know what the House of Commons is. A hundred members of that House might belong to the United Service Club or the Athenaeum or anything else you please. These hundred members might discuss the measures actually before the House in their club; but this could never make the club to be the House; whereas in their true position with the Speaker in the midst a much less number would constitute a House. It is exactly the same principle here. What constitutes God's assembly? "Two or three" gathered unto the Lord's name. He has been pleased to bring it down to the point described, with the fullest possible stamp of His approval and authority.

On the other hand suppose ten thousand Christians meeting simply as Christians—is that enough? I can conceive an assembly of professing, yea, real Christians; and yet there would be no more reason to call them God's assembly than to consider any number of members at their club the House of Commons. It is not the fact of being Christians that constitutes God's assembly, but their being gathered unto the name of the Lord. The practical point for us is whether we are gathered to the name of Christians merely, or to the name of Christ. If the former, you must accept of any evil thing into which the enemy succeeds in dragging Christians. For if the man be a Christian, I must receive him, spite of evil he is doing or sanctioning. But no! the question is, Does he call upon the Lord out of a pure heart? The exclusion of this word of God has widely overrun Christendom to the incalculable injury of souls, and never more than now, when men practically put Christians in lieu of Christ, the consequence of which is confusion and every evil work.

Whereas if the Lord have His place and be the centre to which I come, I have then in His name a ground and rallying point to which I can claim, with the most entire humility, every saint in the world—yea, I could not and ought not to rest in my spirit as long as one that belongs to Him is outside. What! even those under discipline, or avoided for grave causes? Yes, every one; not of course to receive them with known evil upon them, but yet to desire themselves, what is contrary to Christ being judged and removed.

The Lord make us steadfast and give us to feel that the lowliest spirit becomes us! How can we boast of ceasing to do evil we ourselves have done? May we look to Him increasingly! He who has brought us out has compelled us to prove by our own difficulties the true state of the church; but He has turned to profit our very mistakes, though in a humbling way. He has used the storm, as it were, to purge the hazy air, and displayed more clearly than ever the central place of His own name for our gathering together no less than our salvation.

Thus we may leave all fears and anxieties. If the Lord be our helper, why fear? What will man do? Then, as for charges of sectarianism or presumption or disorder, it were easy indeed to show that those are really guilty who are quick to raise and scatter them. We know that scripture condemns every church association that is not based on and governed by the name of Christ. It is not a mere question of wrongs here or there; but are they Christians gathered to the name of Christ? Neither is it a question of the amount of evil? for what did not slip in at Corinth through ignorance and unwatchfulness? The refusal to judge known evil is no doubt fatal. But supposing the absence of everything gross, the true question is, Are we where the Lord would have us be? Then happy are we, if but "two or three" thus: were we ten millions anywhere else, all must be wrong, because Christ is not the acknowledged and exclusive centre ecclesiastically. He who is the only adequate and rightful object for all the saints on earth deigns to be the centre of but "two or three", as He says, that are "gathered together unto his name".

Notes

LECTURE 2: "ONE SPIRIT"

[1].   That "the different denominations" present a state of things directly at variance with "one body and one Spirit" is too plain to call for argument with those who are used to bow to scripture, and to judge present facts by it. How painful then it is to read such sentiments as these in the recent words (June, 1869) of one whom I cannot but love and esteem for his work's sake! "I sometimes think that these will continue for ever. They are of no hurt to the church of God (!) but a great blessing (!); for some of them take up one point of truth which is neglected, and others take up another; and so between them all the whole of truth is brought out (!); and it seems to me that the church is even more one (!) than if all the various sections were brought together into one grand ecclesiastical corporation [who contends for this but a Papist or Puseyite?]; for this would probably feed some ambitious person's vanity, and raise up another dynasty of priestcraft like the old Babylon of Rome. Perhaps it is quite as well as it is; but let each body of Christians keep to its own work, and not sneer at the work of others." Alas! the word of God does not

occur in all this reasoning of unbelief (though in a believer); but as usual the very publication in which it occurs is a witness that this justification of sin is as hollow as its profession of love and order. For a large portion is devoted to sneering at the only Christians who at this time are seeking to give practical effect to their faith in the "one body and one Spirit". With much, very much, of the paper on "Order Heaven's first Law" I go so heartily that I am the more grieved to notice, in however friendly a spirit, such flagrant inconsistency both in principle and in practice. Let us rather humble ourselves for our common sin, seek to walk in obedience and love while waiting for the Lord Jesus, but never abuse the grace of God to deny His truth which condemns our ways.

LECTURE 3: THE ASSEMBLY AND MINISTRY

[2].   It has been objected that some editors, as Lachmann and others, have omitted τῇ ἐκκλησίᾳ here in deference to the Sinai, Vatican, Alexandrian, and Rescript of Paris, and a few juniors, with the Vulgate, Coptic, Æthiopic, and Armenian versions; but all the other uncials and cursives, with the Syriac, Arabic, and Slavonic versions, not to speak of early citations, accept the word; and these were followed by Griesbach, Scholz, &c., as well as Bengel hesitatingly. Tischendorf, who had at first rejected the common reading, replaced it in his later editions, though probably ℵ will now incline him once more against it. But it ought to be remembered that even the school of Lachmann, if they reject it, separate ἐπὶ τὸ αὐτό from [Acts] chapter 3:1, so that the passage would make the sense substantially the same as if τῇ ἐκκλησίᾳ, "to the church", were read; namely, "The Lord was adding daily together those that should be saved." Hence in Acts 4:23 it is said of Peter and John,

that when let go, they went to their own company (πρὸς τούς ἰδίους). There was now a new association to which they belonged distinct from the old congregation of Israel; and this beyond a question is formally called ἡ ἐκκλησία in chapter 5:11, not as if it were *then* called into being, but most evidently as already subsisting and known. It is clear then that independently of the phrase in Acts 2:47, "the assembly", in a New Testament sense, did in fact begin at Pentecost, as is confessed by Pearson, Whitby, and others.

[3]. The external authority stands thus. The Alexandrian, the Vatican, the Palimpsest of Paris, and the Sinai MSS. are documents of the highest value, which agree in reading "the church", not "the churches". In this they are supported by the most important cursive extant, now in the British Museum, along with a fair number of others. Of the ancient versions, there is *not one* of first-rate authority which does not confirm the singular—the Peschito Syriac, Coptic, Sahidic, Vulgate, Æthiopic, Armenian, and the Erpenian Arabic. The most ancient Uncial which gives the plural form is that of Laud, in the Bodleian Library, of about the sixth or seventh century, supported by two others of the ninth century, with the mass of cursives, the Philoxenian Syriac, and an Arabic version. But even here it is to be remarked that the weightiest, or Laudean copy, is unquestionably wrong in reading "*all* the churches"; and the others may have been influenced by Acts 16:5. It is certainly easier to suppose that the less usual form might have been changed by scribes to a common type, than that the very old authorities joined in an error, which the crowd of juniors escaped. Ordinarily, the tendency runs in a direction exactly opposite.

[4]. The Congregational Lecture on "the Ecclesiastical Polity of the New Testament" *[London, 1848; 2nd edition, 1854]*, by Dr. S[amuel] Davidson, may be compared with what we have seen in scripture. "Let us now take a church and trace its various proceedings. A number of believers agree to associate together. In a united capacity they resolve to confess Christ, to observe His precepts, and to follow His will. They choose pastors whom they judge to possess the qualifications described in the New Testament. In this way the believer chosen by them becomes an official person as soon as he accepts their invitation" (p. 269). "The compact entered into between the ruler and the ruled may be dissolved by one or both of the parties. The union formed between pastor and people may be severed" (p. 271). "A minister is either the minister of one church, viz., that by which he has been chosen, or else he is not a minister at all. When he ceases to be pastor of a church he ceases to be a minister of the Gospel, till he be elected by another. . . . . He is not made a minister by the act of ordination, but by the people's call, and his acceptance of it, by virtue of which a solemn engagement is entered into; and when the engagement terminates, he ceases to be a minister (!)" (pp. 252, 253). *No* principle seems to me more flatly opposed to God's word than religious radicalism.

LECTURE 4: WORSHIP, THE BREAKING OF BREAD, AND PRAYER

[5].　　Let me give a few extracts from the famous work of an able and moderate man, John Calvin:—"It is here also pertinent to observe, that it is improper for private individuals to take upon themselves the administration of baptism, for it, as well as the dispensation of the Supper, is part of the ministerial office; for Christ did

not give command to any men or women whatever to baptize, but to those whom He had appointed apostles. And when, in the administration of the Supper, He ordered His disciples to do what they had seen Him do (He having done the part of a legitimate dispenser), He doubtless meant that in this they should imitate His example. The practice which has been in use for many ages, and almost from the very commencement of the church, for laics to baptize in danger of death, when a minister could not be present in time, cannot, it appears to me, be defended on sufficient grounds" (*Inst[itutes]* Book 4, chapter 15 § 20). "For the words of Christ are plain: 'Go ye, therefore, and teach all nations, baptizing them' (Matthew 28:19). Since He appointed the same persons to be preachers of the gospel and dispensers of baptism in the church—'No man taketh this honour unto himself' (Hebrews 5:4), according to the apostle, 'but he that is called of God, as was Aaron'—any one who baptizes without a lawful call usurps another's office" (*Ibid.* § 22). Then, in chapter 17 § 43 of the same book 4, after alluding to some ancient ceremonies in order to dismiss them, he proceeds to say, the Supper "might be administered most becomingly, if dispensed to the church very frequently, at least once a week. The commencement should be with public prayer; next, a sermon should be delivered; then the minister, having placed bread and wine on the table, should read the institution of the Supper, then explain the promise therein left us, and at the same time keep back from communion [excommunicaret] all those who are debarred by the Lord's prohibition. He should, after that, pray that the Lord, according to the kindness in which He bestowed this sacred food on us, would also instruct and form us to receive it with faith and gratitude of mind, and would make us worthy of the feast by

His mercy, since we are not so of ourselves. Here either psalms should be sung, or something read, while the faithful, in due order, communicate at the sacred banquet, the ministers breaking the bread and conveying it to the people. The Supper being ended, an exhortation should be given to sincere faith and confession of faith, to charity and manners worthy of Christians. Lastly, thanks should be offered, and praise of God sung. This done, the Church should be dismissed in peace." How man loves to meddle and legislate! Now, it is instructive to observe that the fullest regulation of the Lord's Supper in scripture occurs in 1 Corinthians, that is, in an epistle written to an assembly where as yet elders were not. Such I believe to have been the case; but even if elders did exist there, the fact remains that absolute silence is kept respecting them, where modern thought would have called them in at once to meet the disorder by a proper administration of the Sacrament. This never occurs to the apostle. The whole assembly are admonished on moral grounds. Such is the divine remedy, not an appeal to the elders if they existed, nor a direction to have them appointed in order to correct the abuse if there were none.

LECTURE 5: GIFTS AND LOCAL CHARGES

[6].   So Archbishop Potter, in the well-known textbook, "A Discourse on Church Government" (pp. 73, 74), if one may, without unkindness, specify a single defaulter out of the crowd. Yet the Archbishop evidently gave up the passage as bearing on ordination. "It cannot be proved that Paul and Barnabas were ordained at this time to be ministers. If they were ordained to any office or ministry, it must be that of apostles, not only because they are presently after this called apostles, before they received any farther ordination, but also because they

were prophets before that time, as shown in one of the preceding chapters [chapter 3]. But this is very unlikely, because this rite of imposing hands, whereby other ministers were ordained [an assumption of the archbishop's without and against Scripture], was never used in making apostles. It was a distinguishing part of their character that they were immediately called and ordained by Christ Himself, who gave them [nay, but 'the disciples' and not apostles only, John 20] the Holy Ghost by breathing on them; but neither He nor any other is ever said to lay hands on them. When a place became vacant in the apostolic college by the apostacy of Judas, the apostles, with the rest of the disciples, chose two candidates, but left to God to appoint whether of them He pleased, to take part of the ministry and apostleship, from which Judas fell. Neither was St. Paul inferior to the rest of the apostles in this mark of honour; for he often asserts himself to be an apostle not of men, nor by man, but immediately, and without the intervention of men, to have been appointed by Jesus Christ, in opposition to those who denied him to be an apostle as was shown in one of the former chapters. But then it will be asked for what end Paul and Barnabas received imposition of hands? To which it may be answered, that this rite was commonly used, both by the Jews and primitive Christians in benedictions. Jacob put his hands on the heads of Ephraim and Manasseh when he blessed them; and, to mention only one instance more, little children were brought to Christ, that He should put His hands on them and bless them. Accordingly, it is probable this imposition of hands on Paul and Barnabas was a solemn benediction on their ministry of preaching the Gospel in a particular circuit to which they were sent by the Holy Spirit's direction. Hence it is called in the next chapter a recommendation to the grace of God for the work of ministering the Gospel to certain cities, which they are said to have fulfilled. So that this rite was not their ordination to the apostolic office, because the end for which it was given is here said to be fulfilled, whereas their apostolic office lasted as long as their lives. And therefore, Paul and Barnabas seem only now to have had a particular mission to preach the Gospel in a certain limited district, in the same manner as Peter and John were sent by the college of apostles to Samaria, to confirm the new converts and settle the Church there."—*Crosthwaite's (or the Seventh) Edition, pp.* 201, 202.

This is substantially true and sound, far preferable to Calvin's remarks *(Inst[itutes]* Book 4, chapter 3 § 14): "Why this separation and laying on of hands, after the Holy Spirit had attested their election, unless that ecclesiastical discipline might be preserved in appointing ministers by men? God could not give a more illustrious proof of His approbation of this order, than by causing Paul to be set apart by the Church, [?] after He had previously declared that He had appointed him to be the Apostle of the Gentiles. The same thing we may see in the election [?] of Matthias. As the apostolic office was of such importance that they did not venture to appoint any one to it of their own judgment, they bring forward two, on one of whom the lot might fall, that thus the election might have a sure testimony from heaven, and at the same time the policy of the Church [?] might not be disregarded." The truth is, as to the case of Matthias, it was before the mission of the Holy Ghost, and there was no question of the Church's policy or election either; but by the lot the choice between the two was cast, in the Jewish form (Proverbs 16:33), into the sole disposal of the Lord.

[7].   Dr. Ellicott goes so far as to think with Hammond, as well as De Wette, &c., that the words refer to the χειρο θεσία on the absolution of penitents and their re-admission to church-fellowship. This seems to me too special in another direction.

[8].   Dr. Crawford ("Presbyterianism Defended", pp. 34, 35, note) says that the distinction is groundless, and that the one preposition no less than the other often signifies the instrumental cause of a thing! The University of Edinburgh may blush for such a statement from its Professor of Divinity. In Acts 15:4, μετ᾽ αὐτῶν means "in connexion with them", *not* "by them", like δι᾽ αὐτῶν in verse 12.

NOTE ON ACTS 14:23

[9].   "Refert enim Lucas constitutos esse per ecclesias presbyteros à Paulo et Barnaba: sed rationem vel modum simul notat, quum dicit factum id esse suffragiis, χειροτονήσαντες, inquit, πρεσβυτέρους κατ᾽ ἐκκλησίαν. Creabant ergo ipsi duo: sed tota multitudo, ut mos Græcorum in electionibus erat, manibus sublatis declarabat quem habere vellent" (Genevæ, 1618).

LECTURES ON THE CHURCH OF GOD

* 9 7 8 0 9 0 1 8 6 0 5 0 7 *